ALONG THE KAW

A Journey Down the Kansas River

Photographs by Craig Thompson

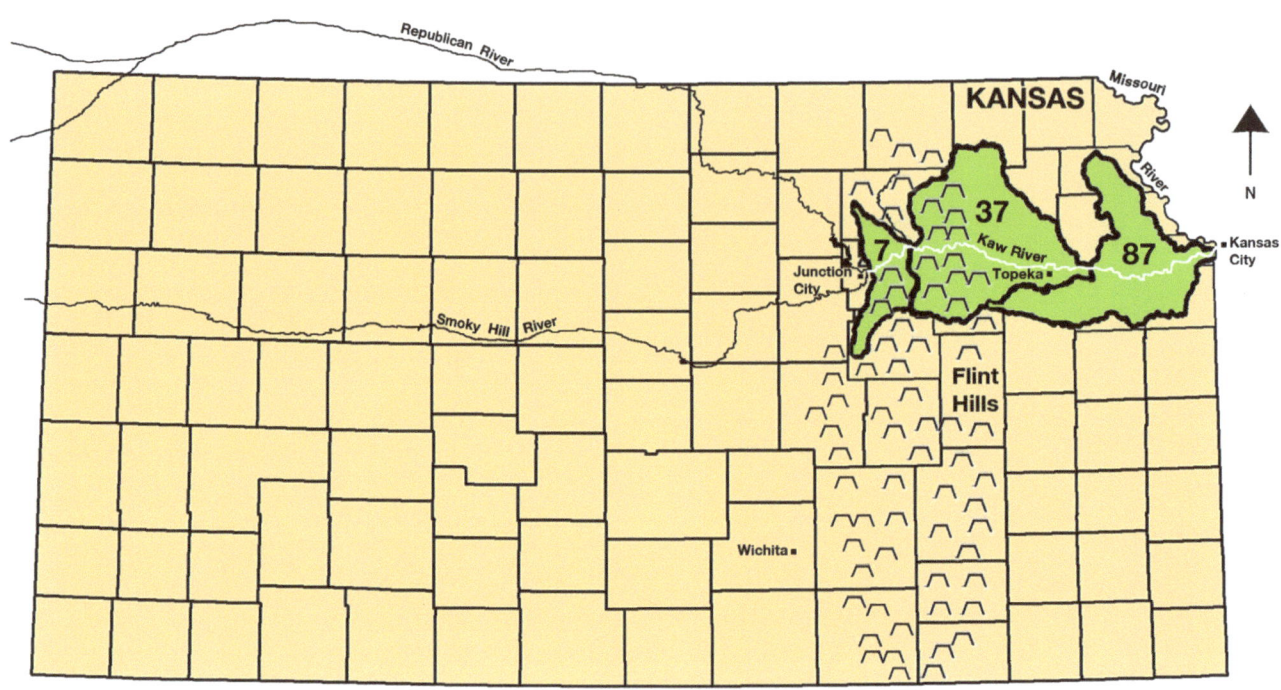

TABLE OF CONTENTS

PREFACE

Along the Kaw: A Journey Down the Kansas River has seventy-three
beautiful photographic images presented in three chapters. Each chapter
is devoted to one of the three watersheds of the Kaw's main stem: the Upper
Kaw, the Middle Kaw, and the Lower Kaw. At the beginning of each chapter
there is an illustrated watershed map showing the Kaw and its major tributaries,
counties and towns. The Kaw has been subdivided into numbered segments
on these maps. For readers interested where the images were made on the
river, a segment number is provided on each page that has a photograph.
These segment numbers correspond to the numbered segments in
the chapter maps.

~~~~~~~~~~~

This book is dedicated to the memory of my father, Gerald Thompson, whose
fascination with the great outdoors sparked my love for nature and to my mother,
Hattie Thompson, who has always encouraged me to pursue my interests. Special
thanks go to Hollis Officer for lending me his scanner, Mike and Laura Calwell
for introducing me to the Kaw, and Steve Cringan for printing my beautiful
Kaw River cards. Thanks are due to Sarah Bent, Bill Dodd, Rolland Love
and the many contributing authors for their help and great comments.

4

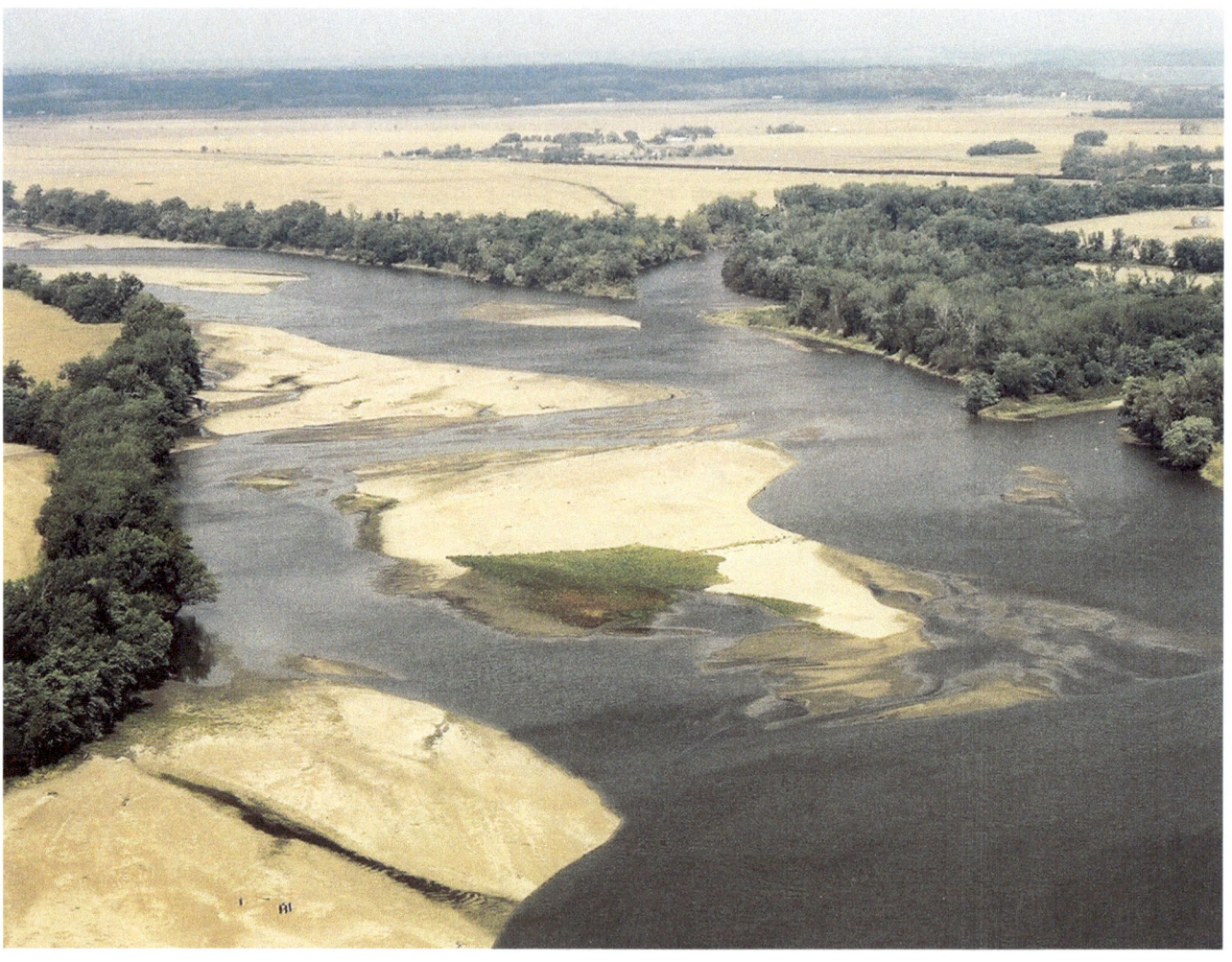

Shallow side channels and large sandbars are characteristic of unimpaired segments of the Kaw.
Kaw (Kansas River) at Lecompton
Segment 23, Douglas County

INTRODUCTION

I like experiencing the sights and sounds I find on the Kaw. There are beautiful sunrises, sunsets, and thousands of stars in the night sky when camping on a sandbar. While floating down the river, I like listening to the simple sounds of rippling water, fish splashing, and the rattling song of the Belted Kingfisher. I feel automatically better when I experience this connection with this moving, living river. The Kaw has inspired me to create this book with photographic images I have taken over the years.

The images in this book were all photographed along the river's 173-mile length from Junction City to Kansas City, Kansas. Many of the images are brought to life by comments from various people whose lives have been touched in some way by the Kaw. Throughout the book, I have matched comments by thirty-nine contributing authors with images of the natural Kaw and images of the recreational Kaw - kayaking, canoeing, fishing and camping.

This river is a beautiful place to recreate. With more accesses to the river and an official designation as a National Water Trail, the Kaw will offer everyone the opportunity to connect with the sights and sounds that to me are unrivaled by any other experience in the state.

Craig Thompson
Friend of the Kaw

A L O N G   T H E   K A W

6

Note: Segment numbers on each page with a photograph correspond with segment numbers on the chapter maps.

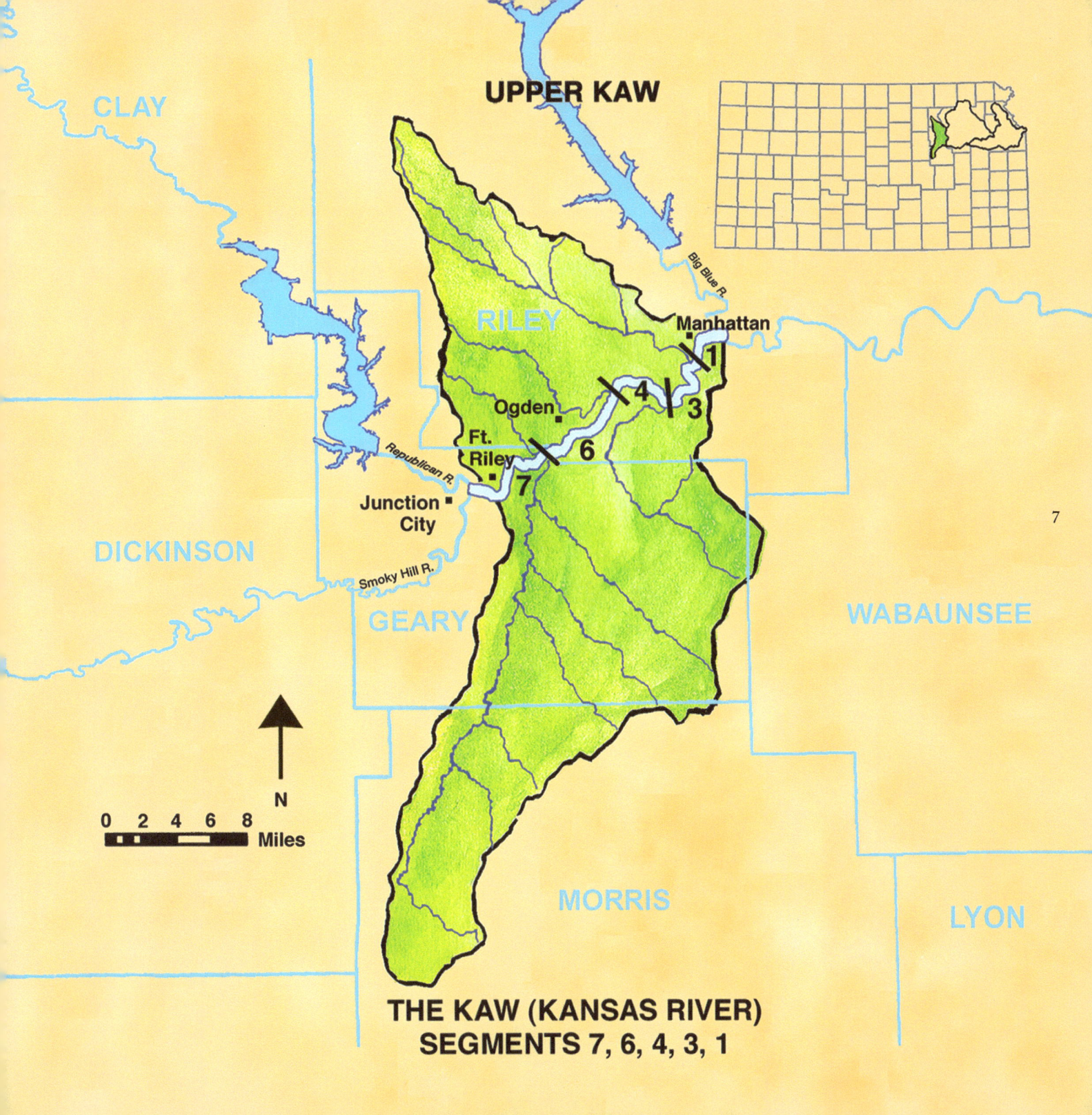

UPPER KAW

CLAY

Big Blue R.

RILEY

Manhattan
1

4
3

Ogden

Ft.
Riley
6

7

Republican R.

Junction
City

DICKINSON

Smoky Hill R.

GEARY

WABAUNSEE

7

N

0 2 4 6 8
Miles

MORRIS

LYON

**THE KAW (KANSAS RIVER)
SEGMENTS 7, 6, 4, 3, 1**

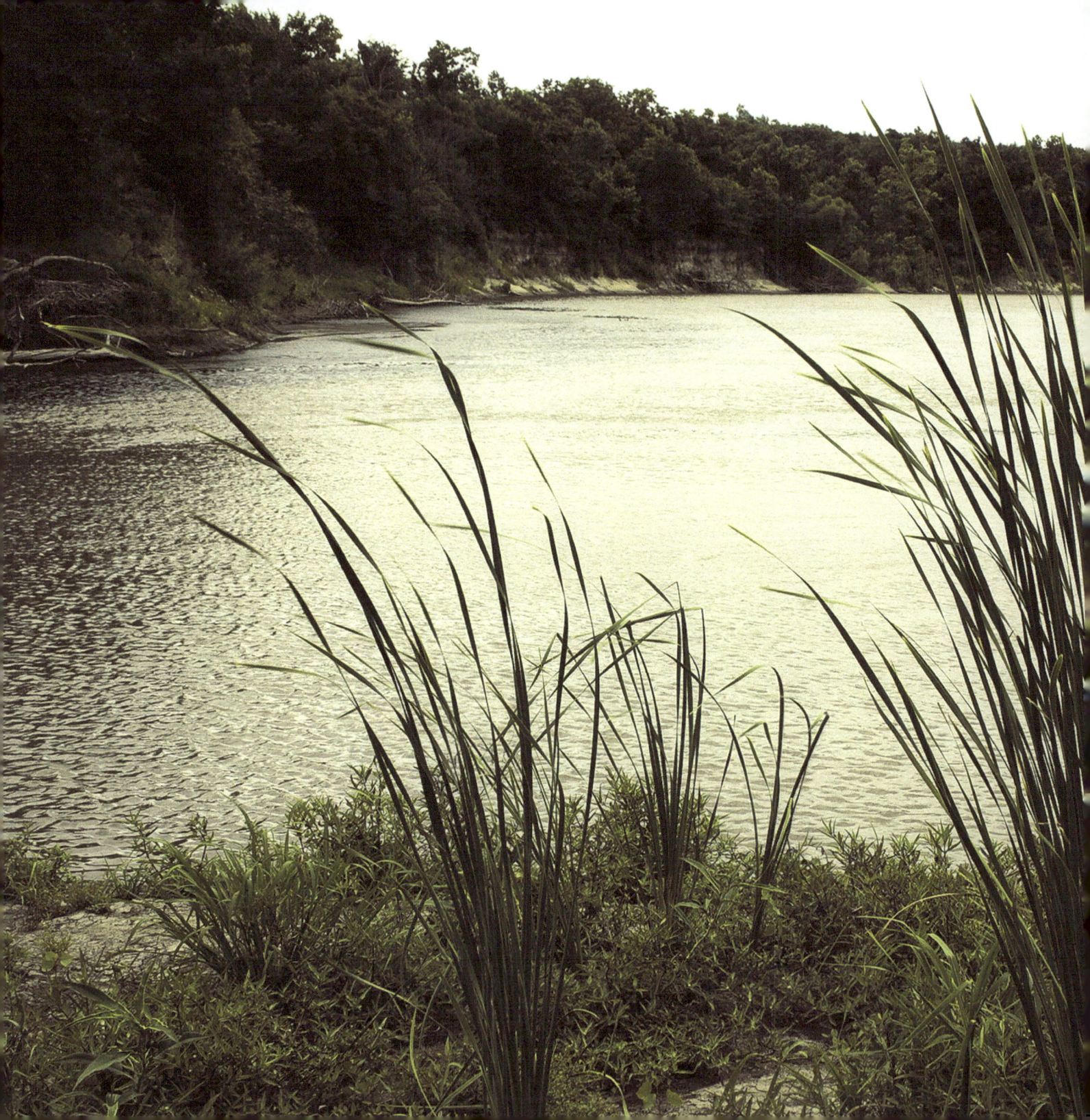

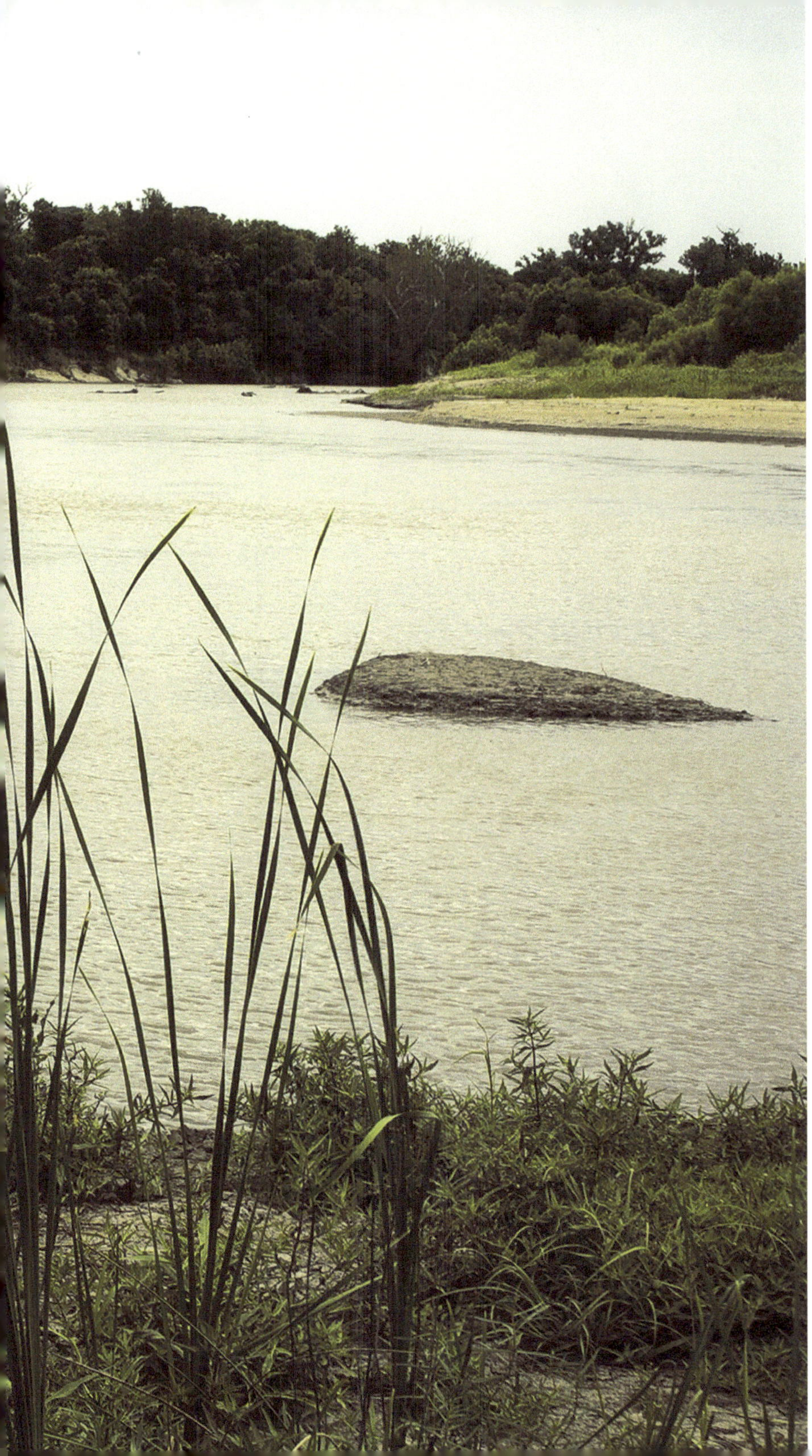

"LET YOUR HEART
follow the river."

- Lance Burr

Kaw at confluence of the
Republican and Smoky Hill
Segment 7, Geary County

"YOU MIGHT SEE RIPRAP, an old tire, or a very old rusted out car now and then, but clearly nature owns the banks."

– Susan Kysela

Tall cottonwood displaying fall color
Segment 7, Geary County

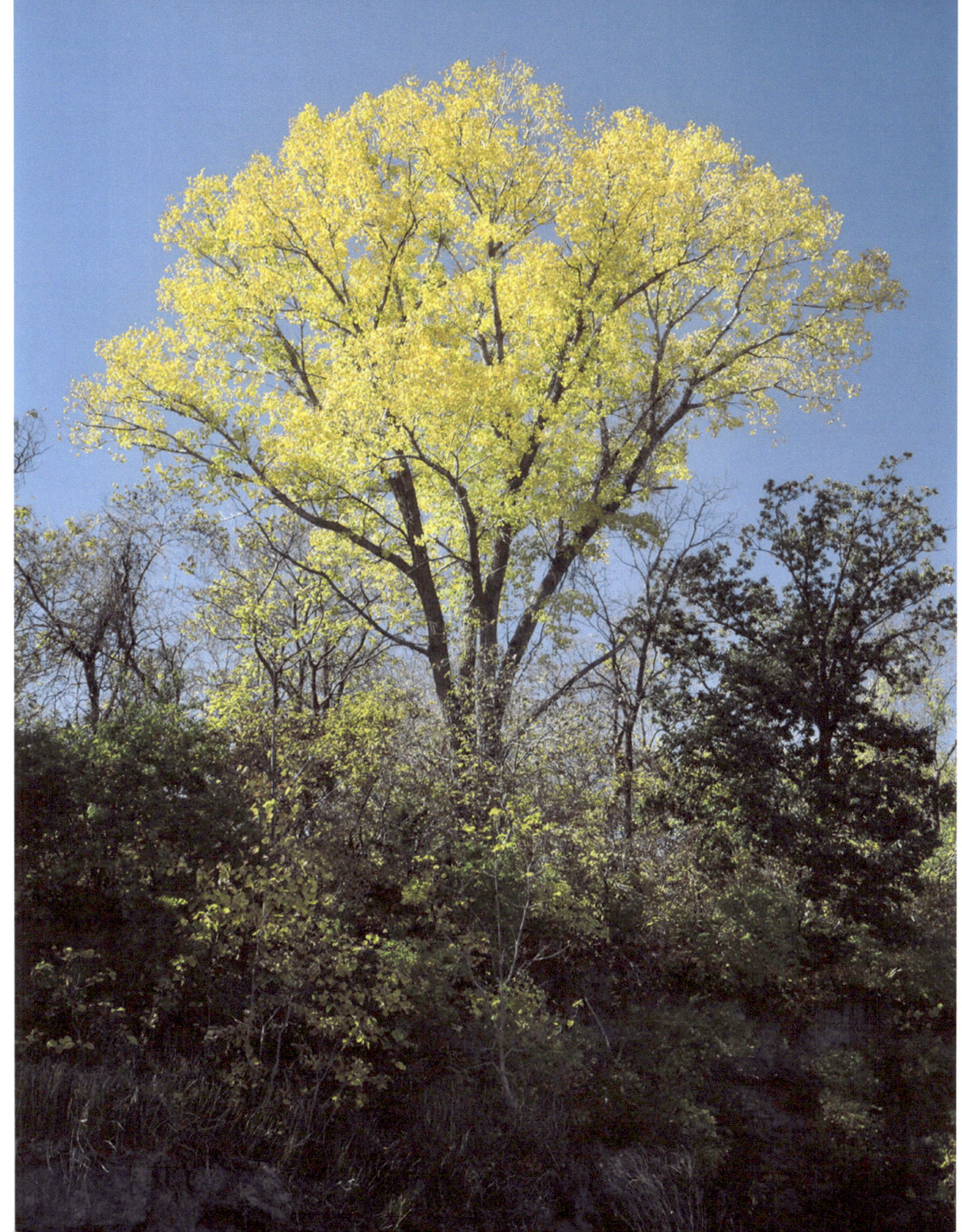

11

12

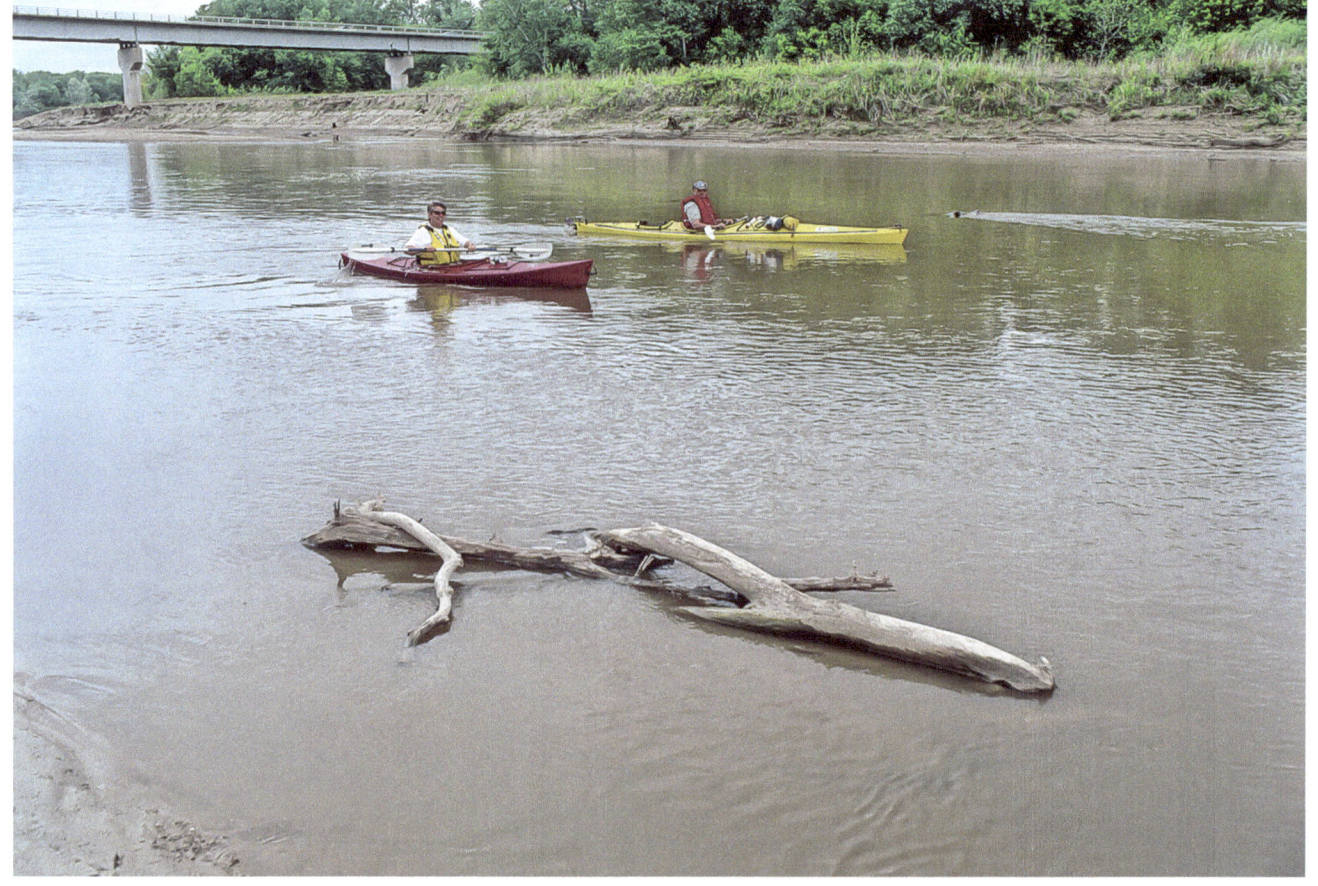

Kayak paddlers near Henry Bridge
Segment 7, Geary County

"OVER THE COURSE of a Kaw float, you develop a strong bond with your boat, the river, and your fellow paddlers."

— Chip Farley

"IT'S ALL ABOUT hangin' out with the "best" people while adventuring on a river. Any number will "do". But I remember the "people" I have floated with almost as much (maybe more) as the "river" itself, no matter "where".

- James E. Alldritt

14

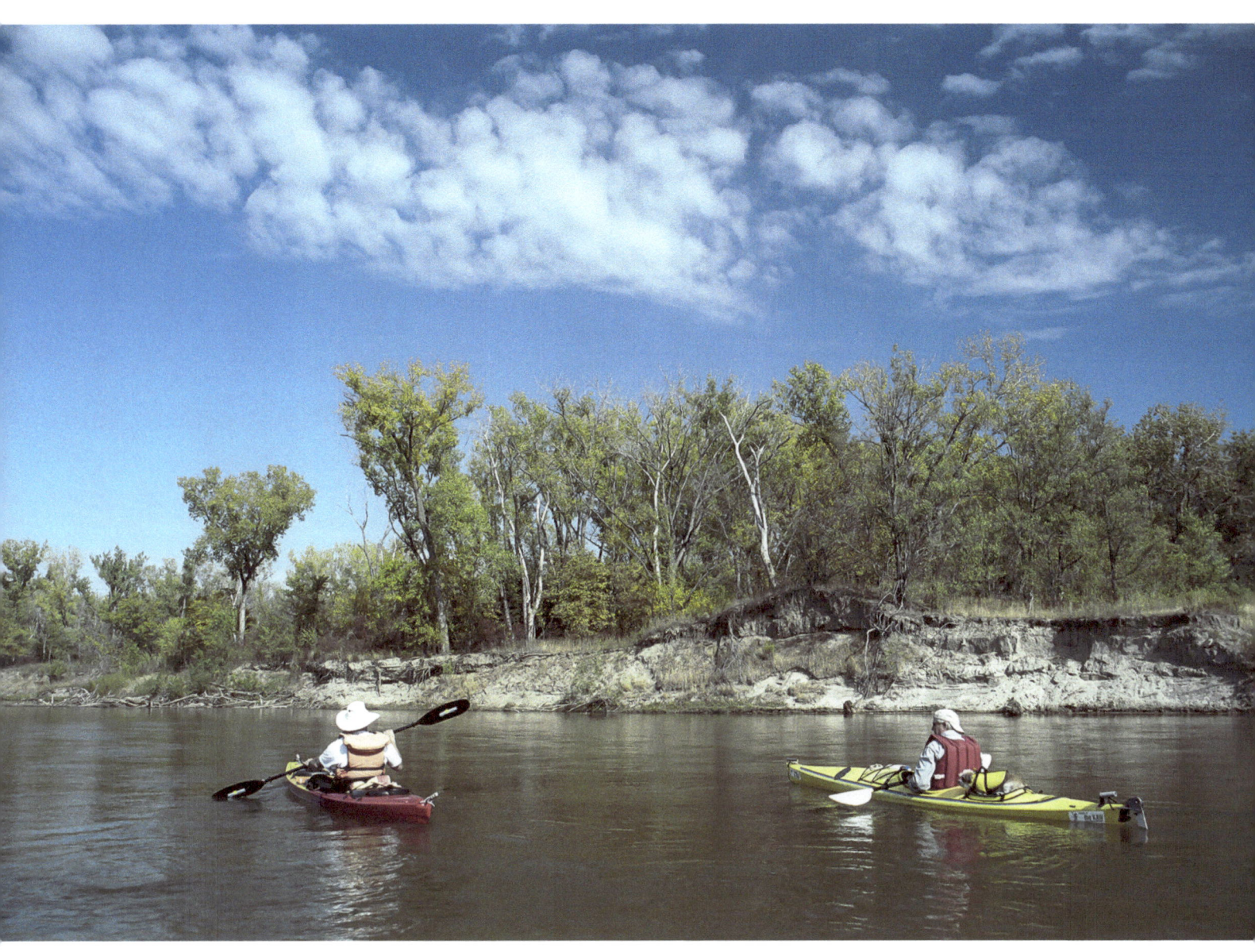

River time
Segment 7, Geary County

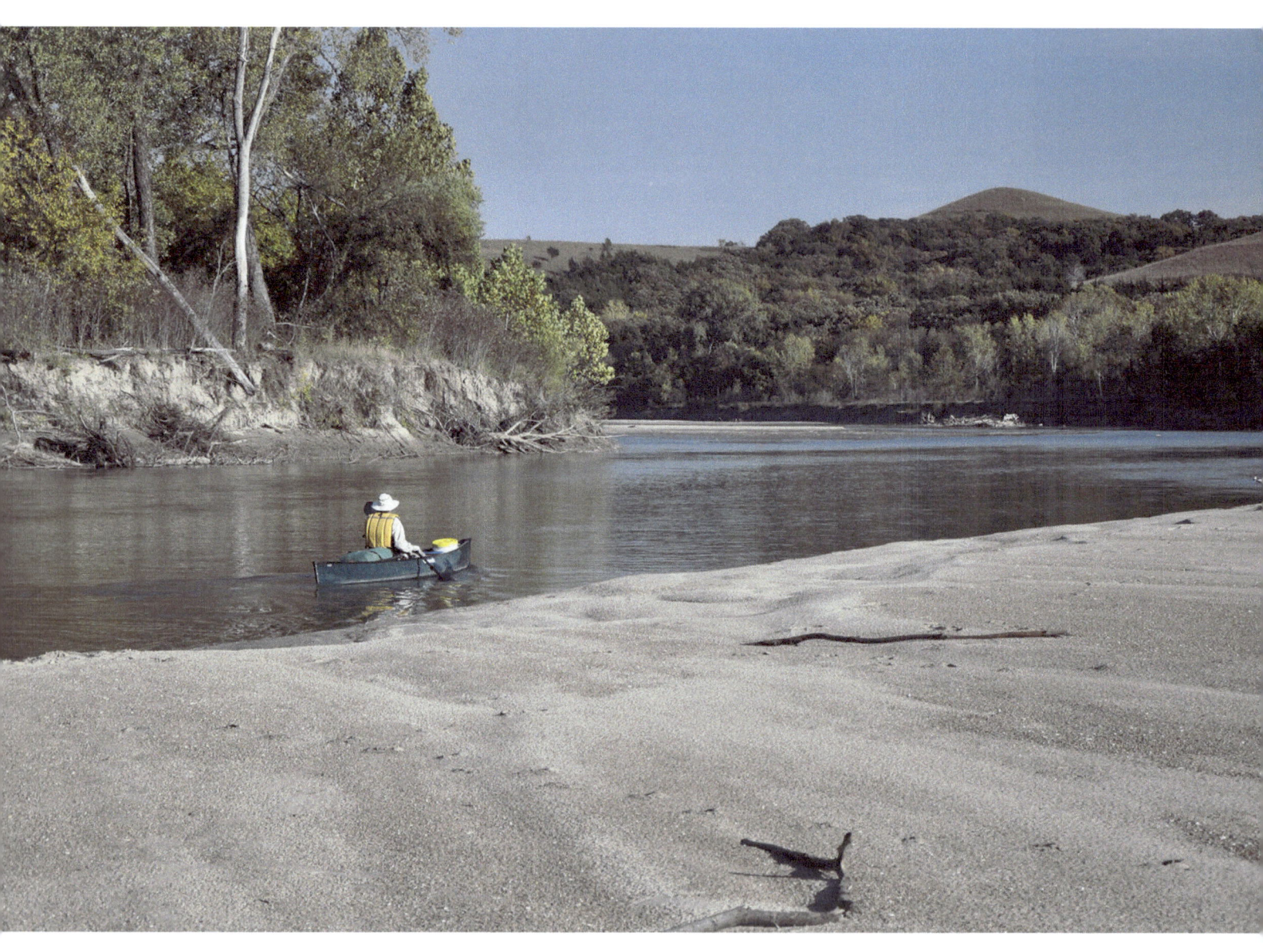

Cruising near Ogden
Segment 6, Riley County

"THE KAW RIVER offers a solitude not found anywhere else in Kansas. You are out in plain site but isolated from roads and traffic. Wildlife is around virtually every bend in the river. You are on your own, unprotected by the confines of an amusement park."

- Roger L. Boyd

"THERE IS SIMPLY nothing more relaxing than sitting around a campfire, swapping stories with friends and sipping a hot drink."

-Erlene Slingsby

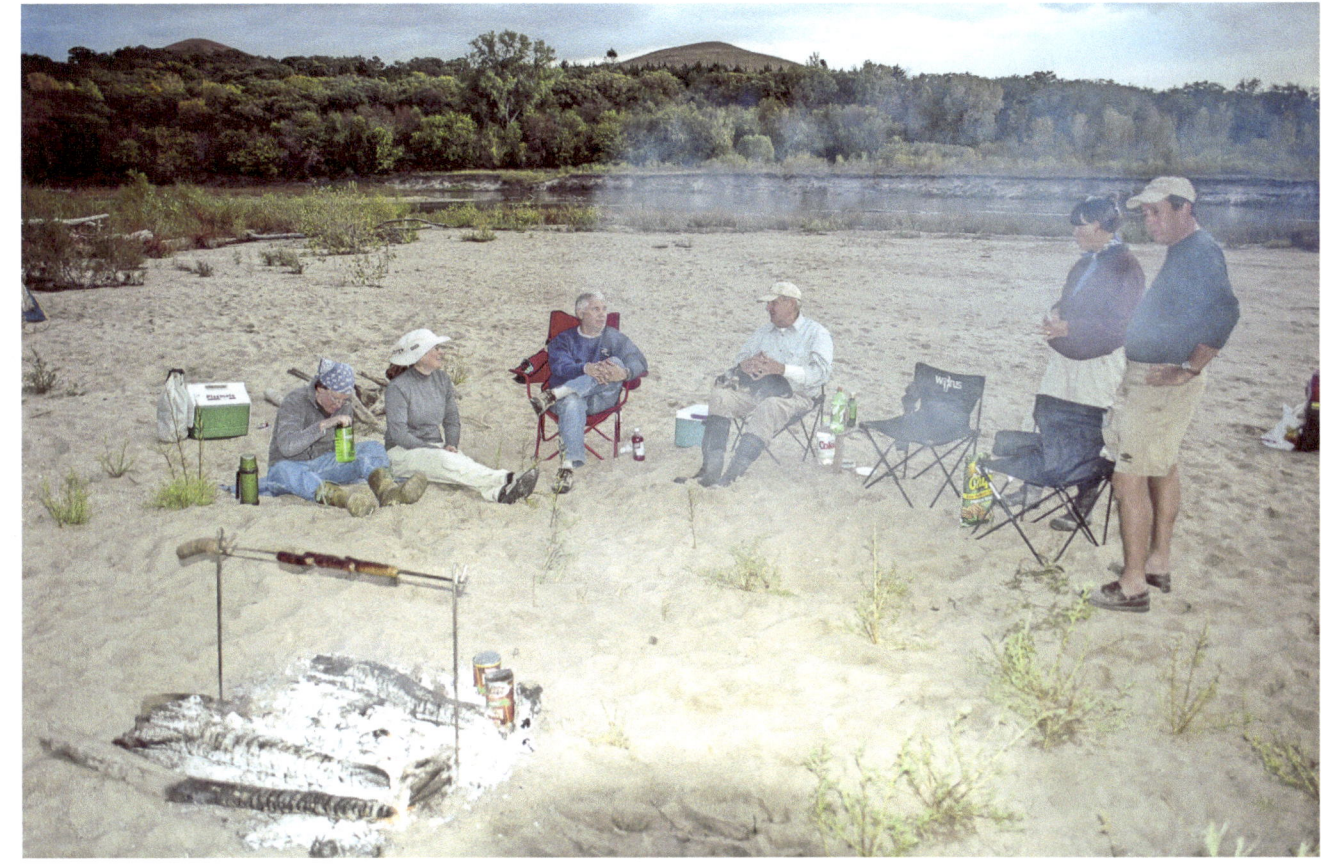

19

Sandbar campfire
Segment 6, Riley County

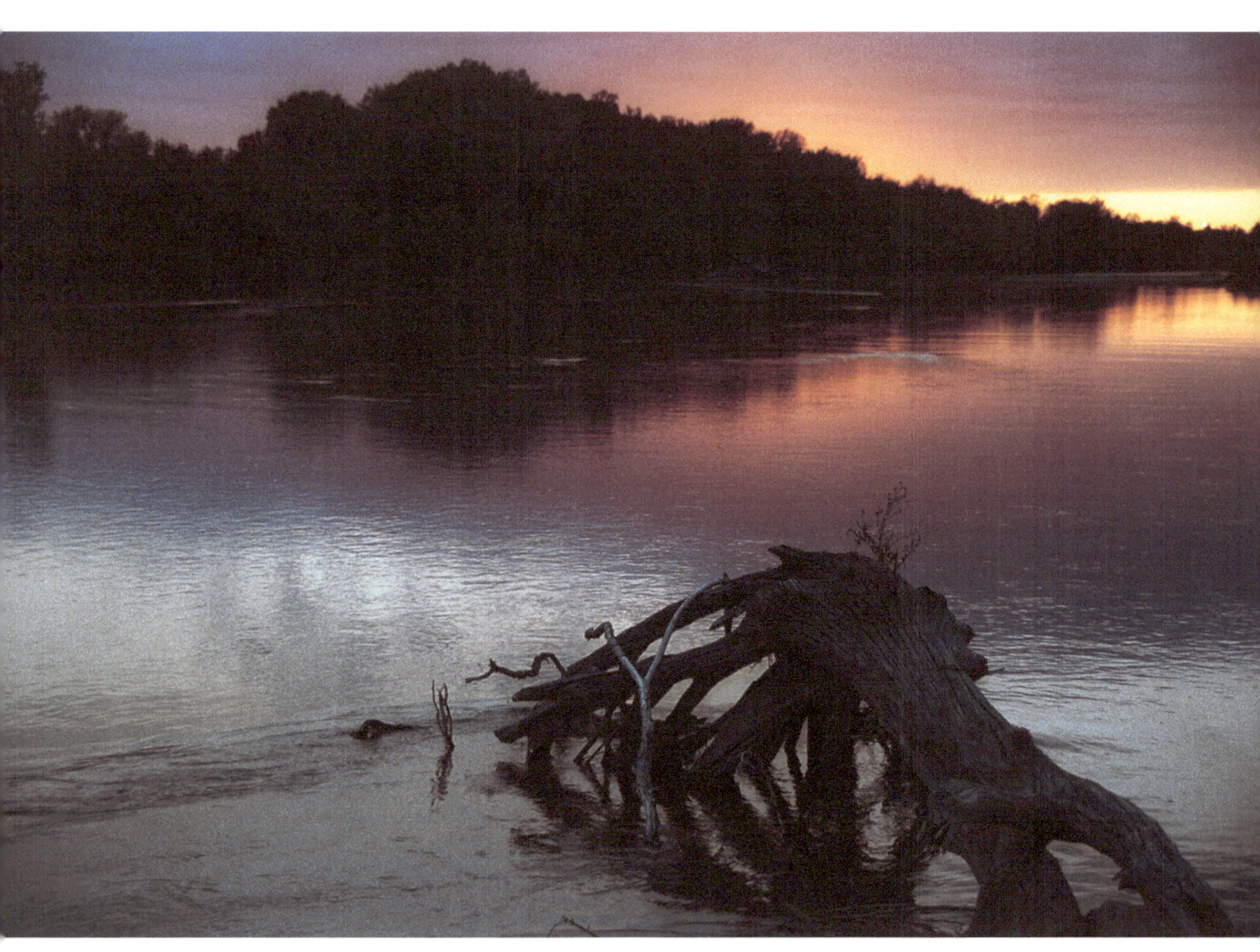

Early evening on the Kaw
Segment 6, Riley County

"THE MOST STRIKING FEATURE of my Kaw River experiences is a sudden awareness that you leave no mark upon the river. The only thing that really matters is that you're there, in that spot, right then. The river moves on and forgets you instantly, but you find yourself grasping for the significance of those single moments and the sights, sounds and textures that went with it.**"**

- Larry Shepard

(overleaf)
Flint Hills morning
Segment 6, Riley County

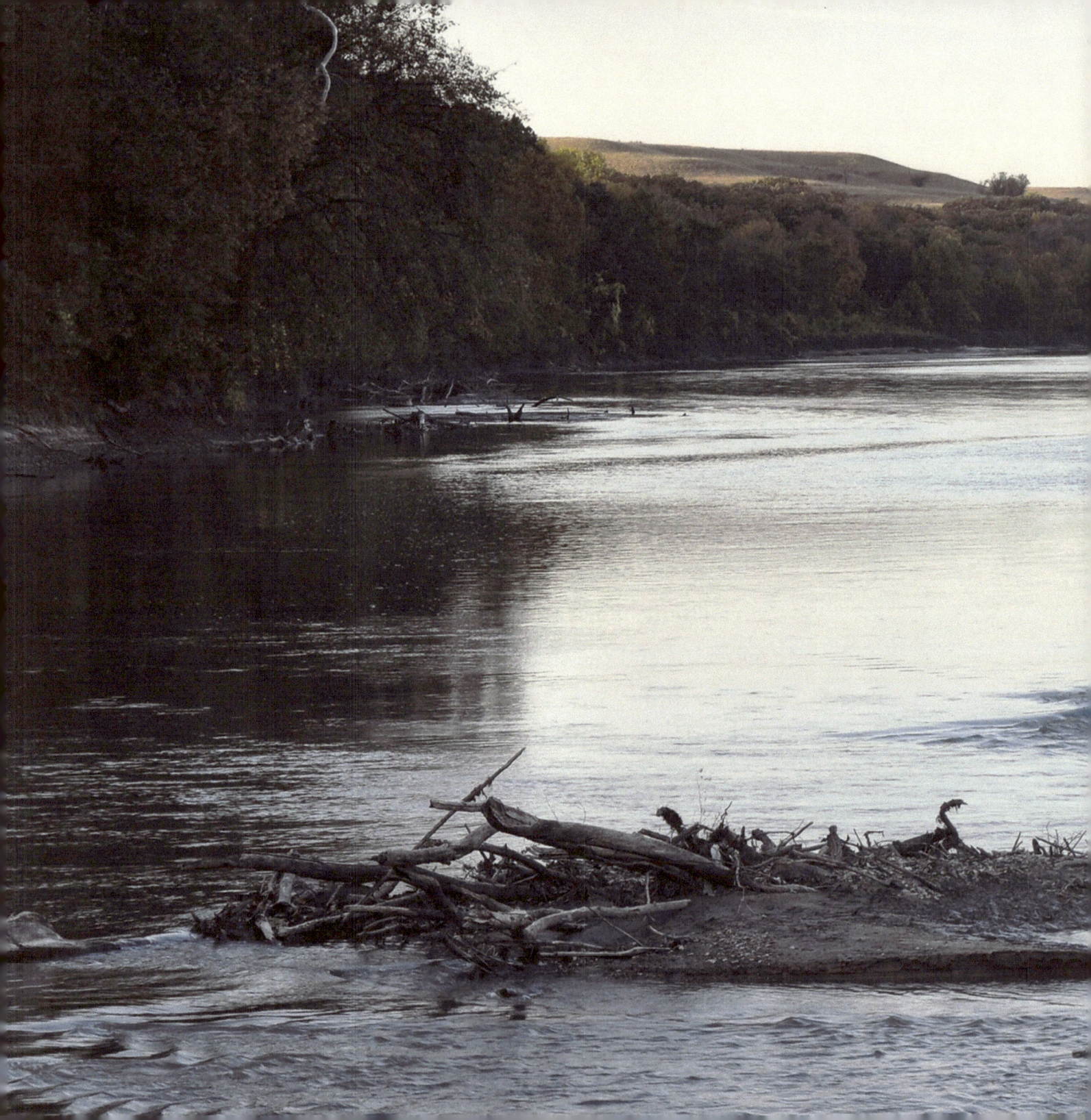

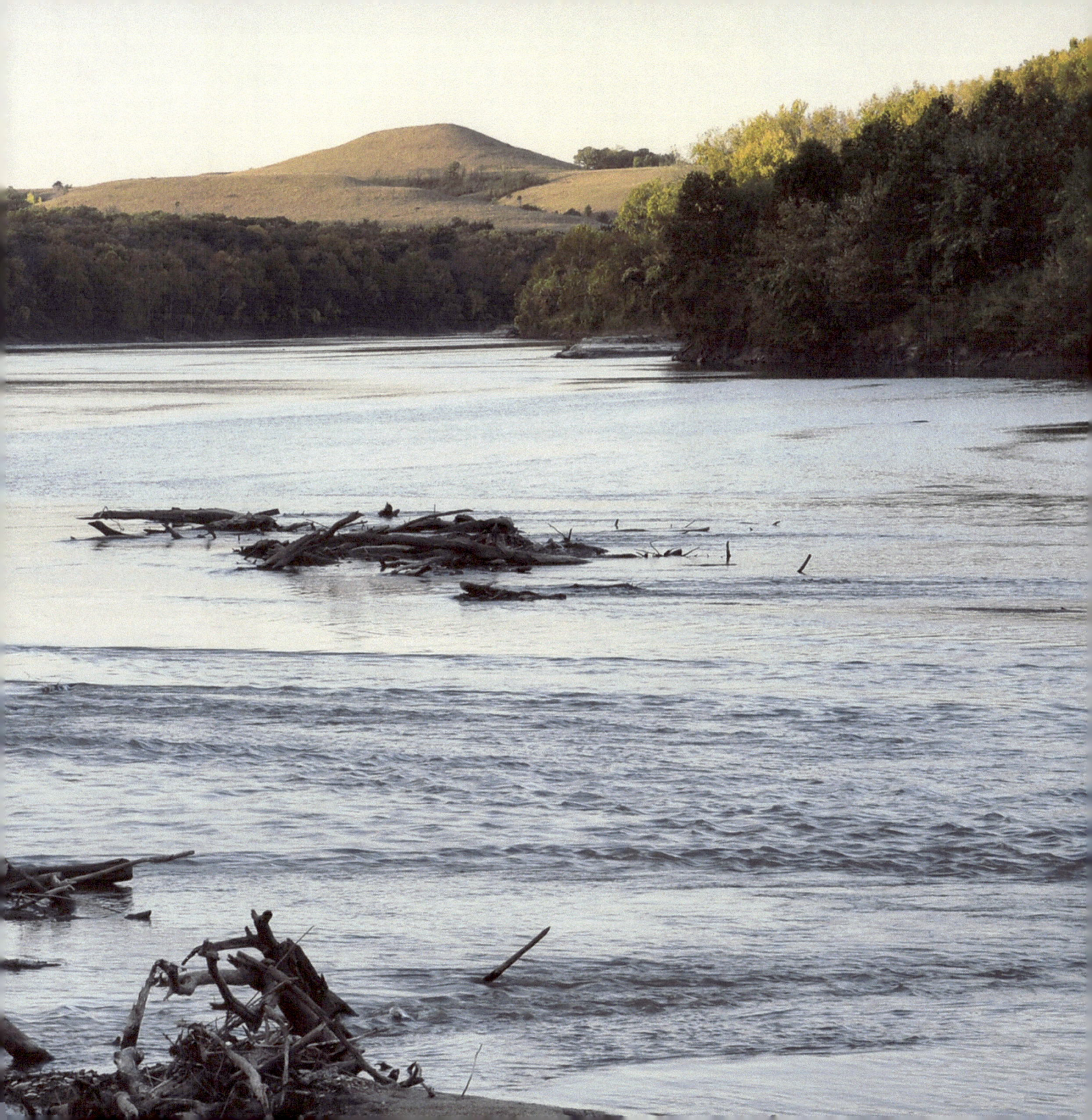

"FALL BRINGS MILD WEATHER

and a kaleidoscope of changing colors in the trees that border and define the river. September through early November are the ideal months for canoeing the Kaw and are the best time of year for introducing its wonders to newcomers.**"**

- Mike Calwell

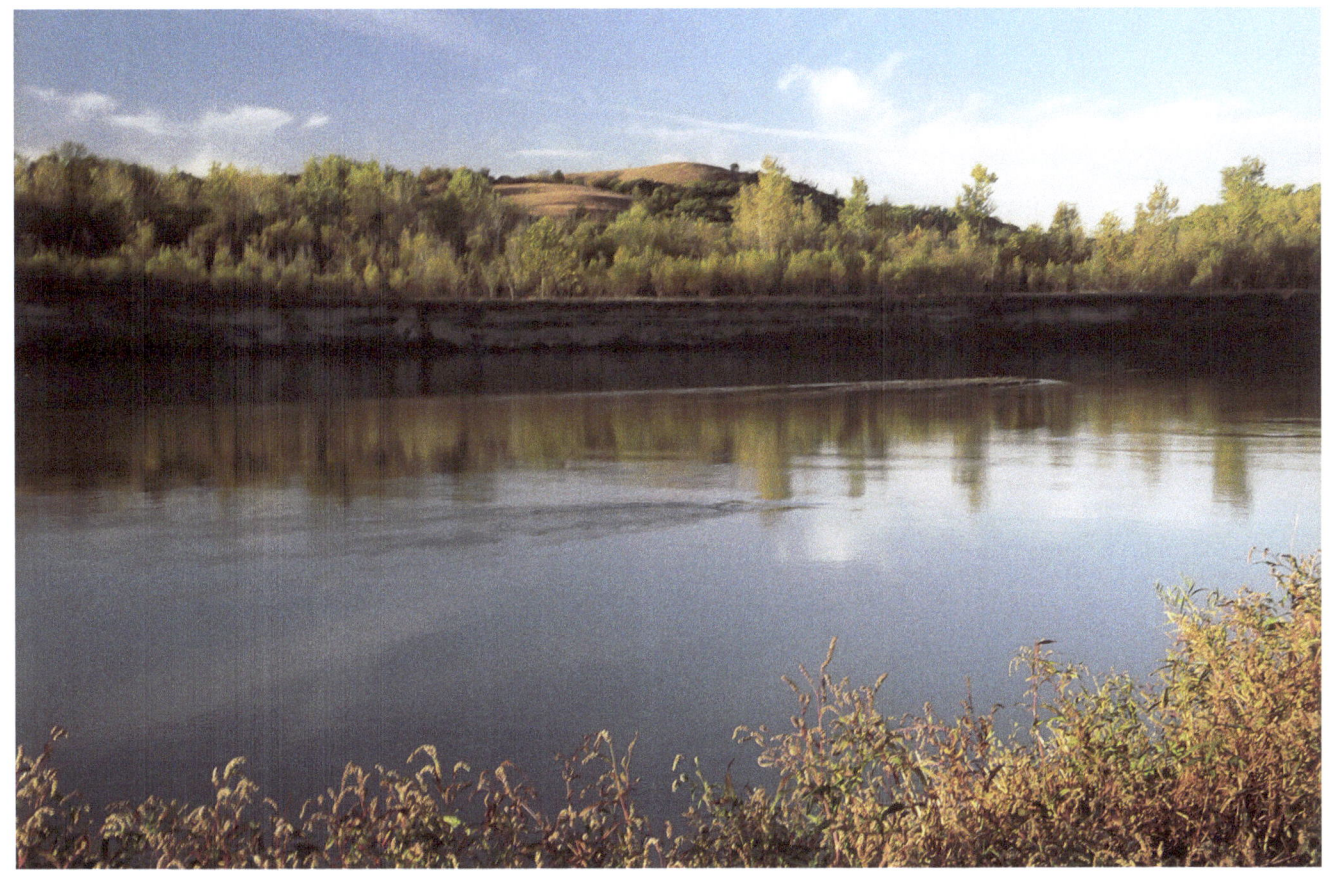

Fall in the Flint Hills
Segment 6, Riley County

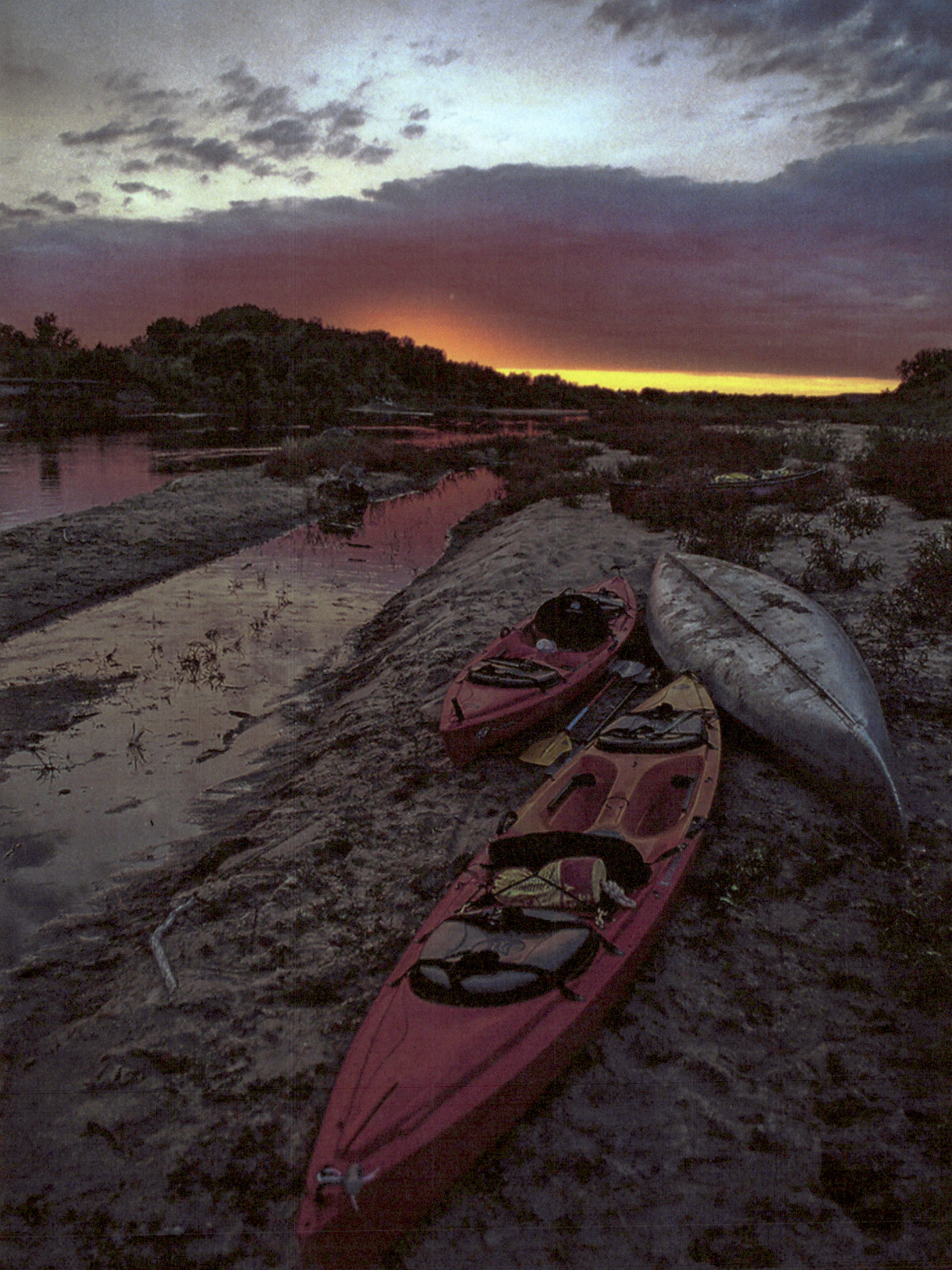

"SUNSET ON THE KAW gives us freedom from the hectic hustle and pressure of everyday life.**"**

– Ron Brann

Sunset over boats
Segment 6, Riley County

"YIPS, BELLOWS, floating conversations
Riding point, picking up drag
Errant, ebullient floaters on the Kaw"

- Mollie Mangerich

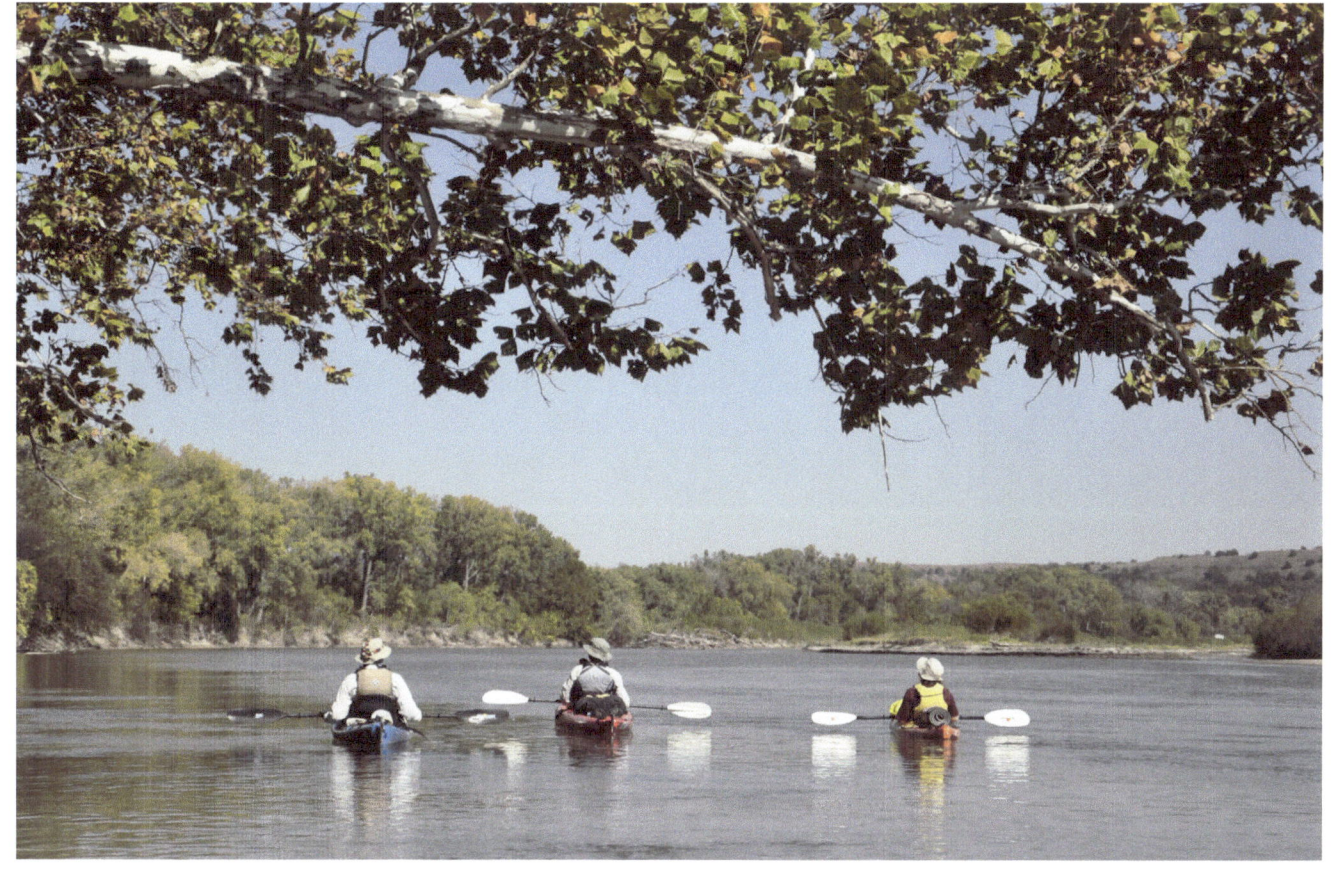

Paddlers share a peaceful moment
Segment 4, Riley County

30

Floating lazily in the Flint Hills
Segment 3, Riley County

"IT'S GREAT with a group of friends - sometimes we paddle close together, pointing out wildlife and other things along the river or in the sky - other times we find ourselves apart, lost in thought, and enjoying a peace not found off the water."

- Bill Cutler

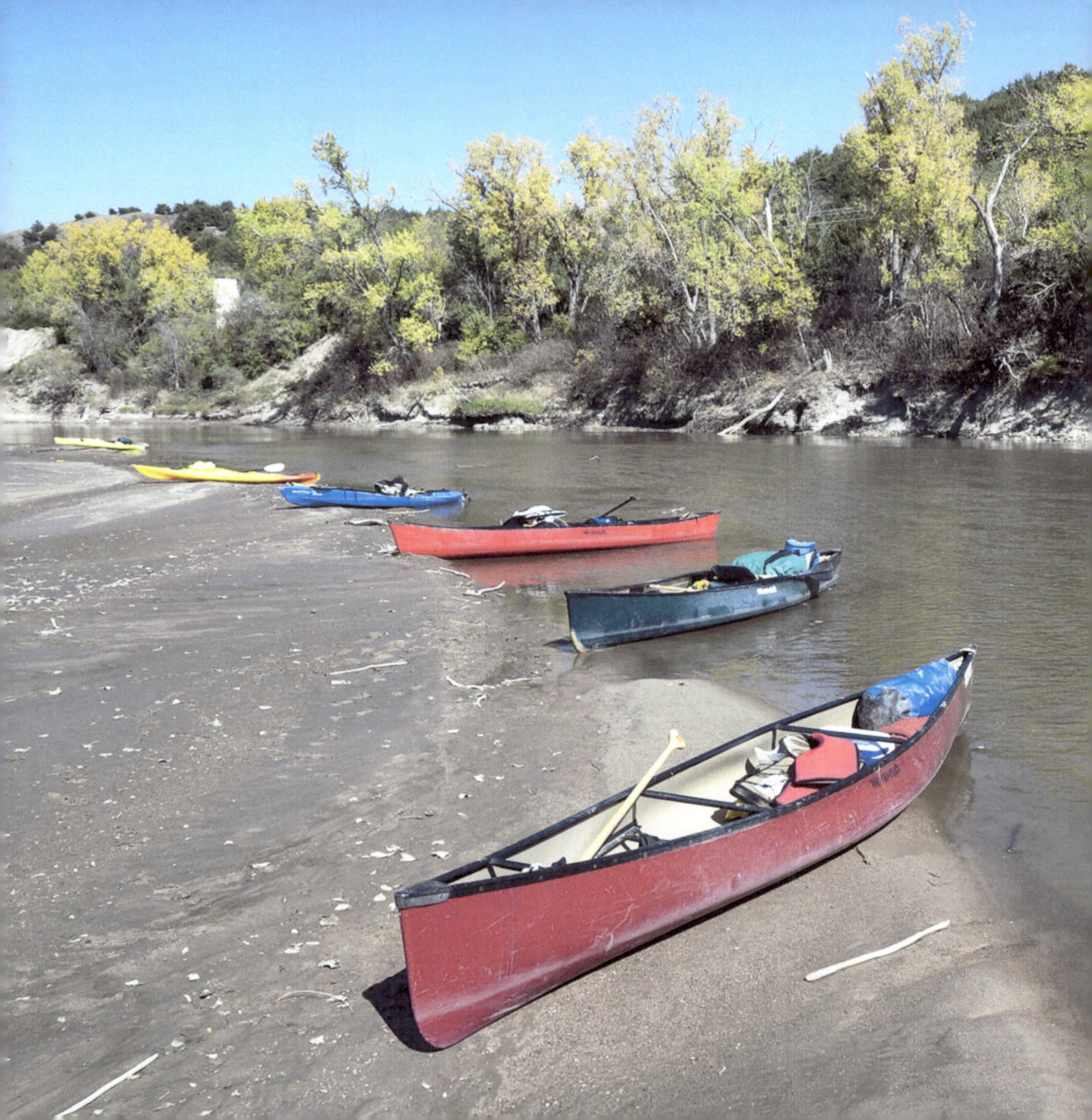

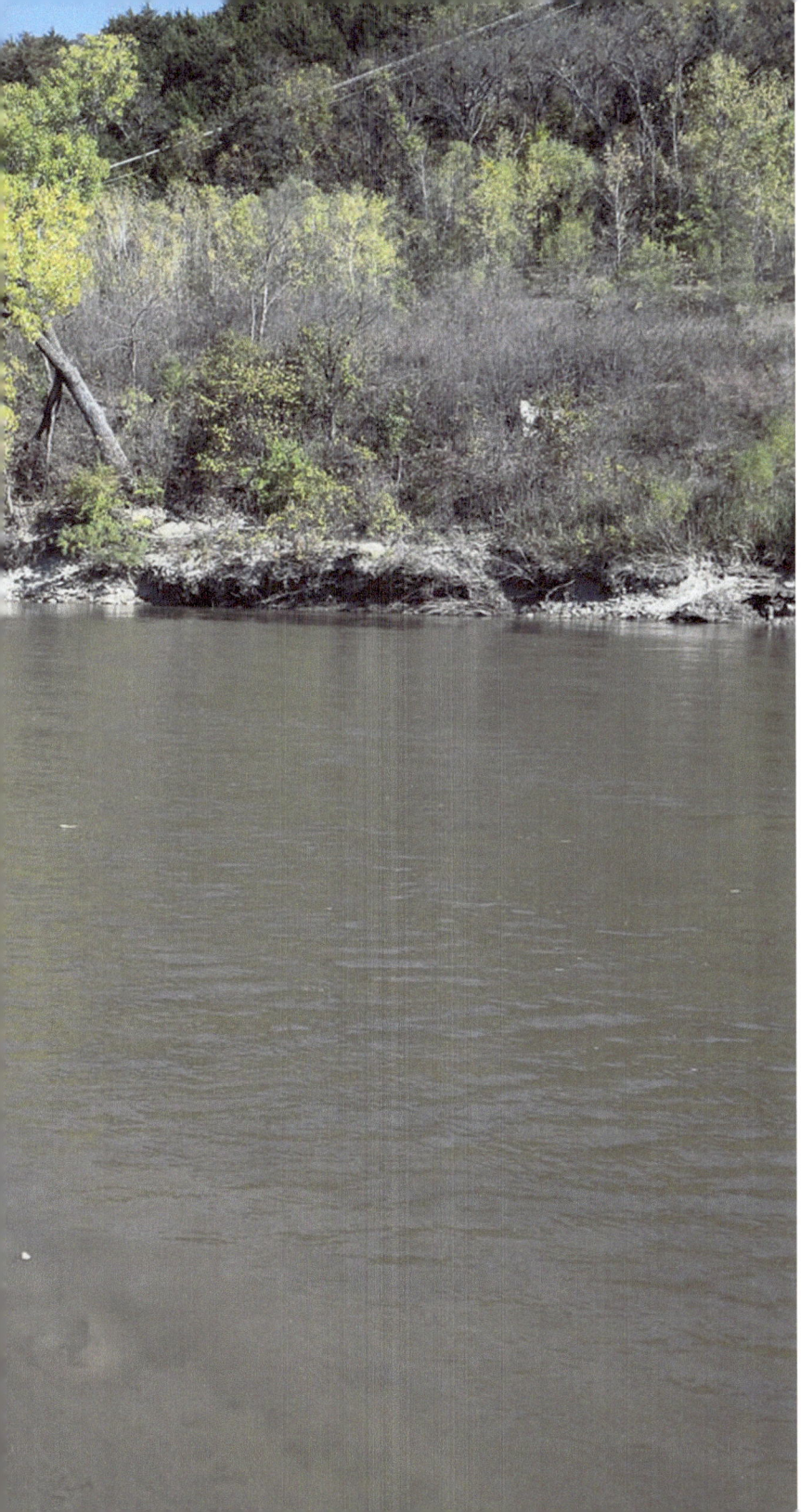

"THE KAW

is usually a slow
moving, shallow river
appropriate for novice
paddlers and family
canoe and kayak
outings.**"**

- Laura Calwell

Boats parked on sandbar
Segment 3, Riley County

"A FEW FRIENDS of mine are what I call adrenalin junkies who live only for the thrill of paddling down scary white water rapids. But most of us saner types are interested in waters of a calmer sort. For us, to pause in an eddy and watch a wading heron patiently waiting for the opportunity to spear a minnow with her lightning bolt beak provides a high degree of suspense and drama."

- Mike Ducey

Great Blue Heron fishing
Segment 1, Riley County

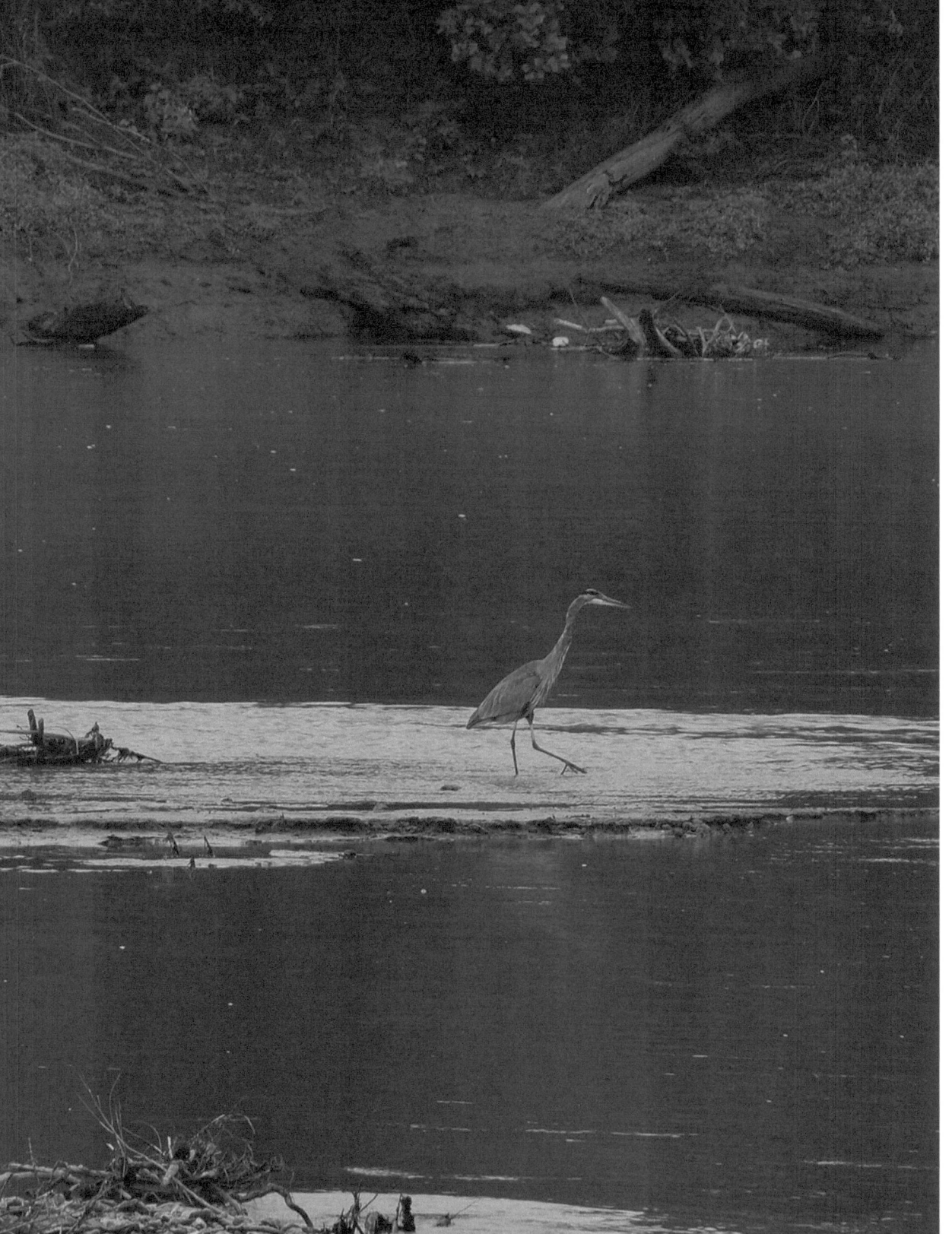

36

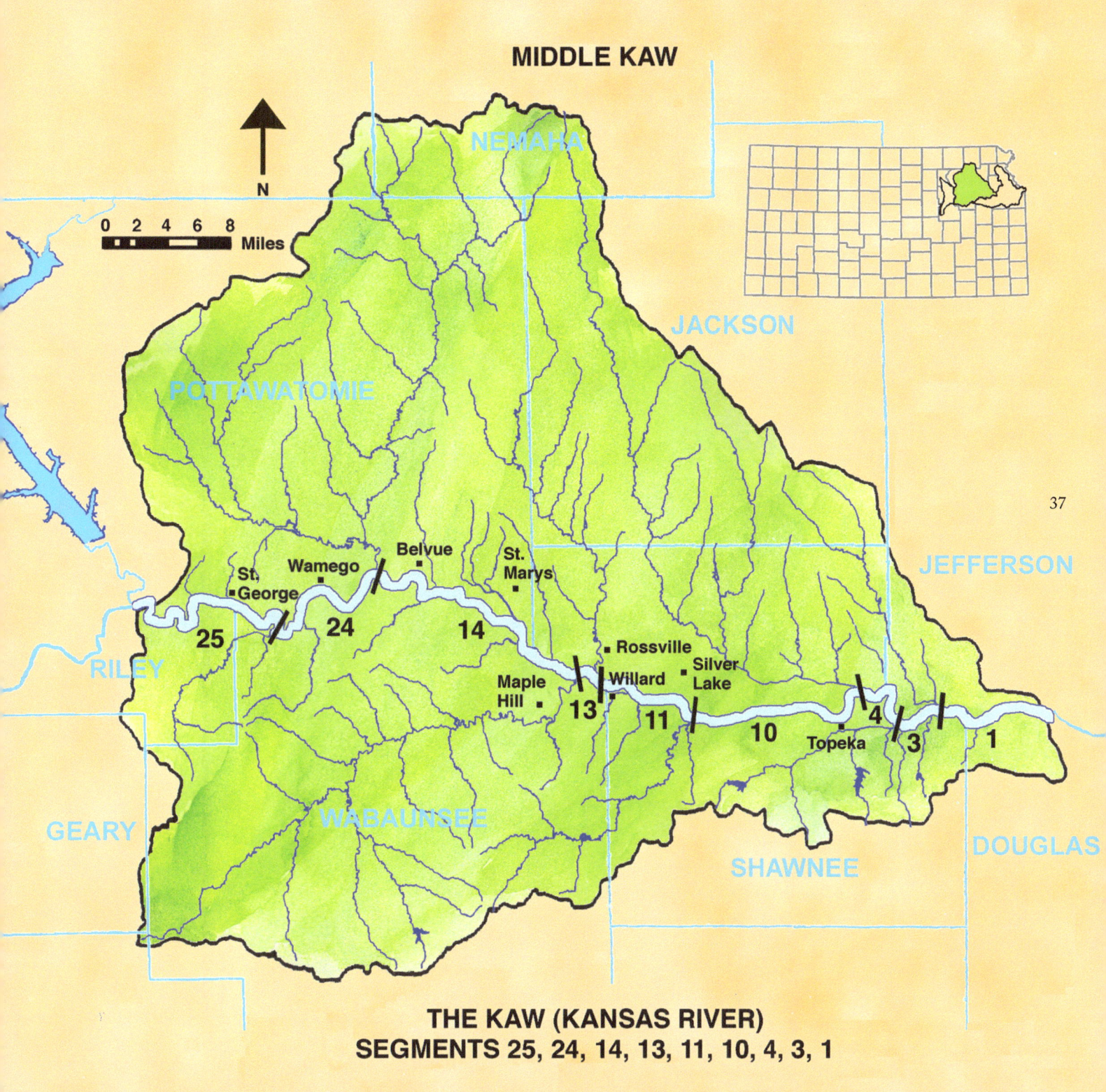

MIDDLE KAW

37

THE KAW (KANSAS RIVER)
SEGMENTS 25, 24, 14, 13, 11, 10, 4, 3, 1

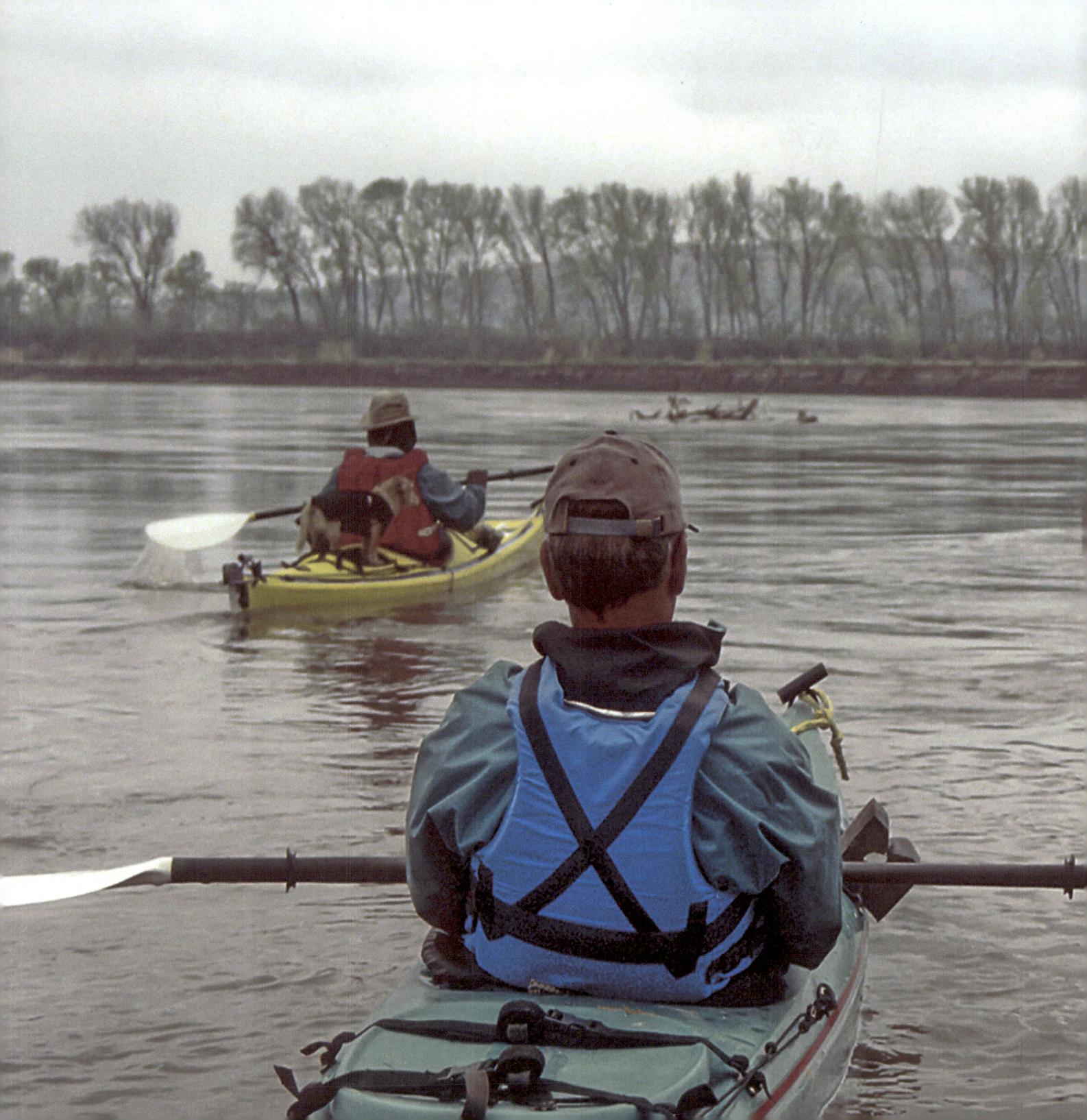

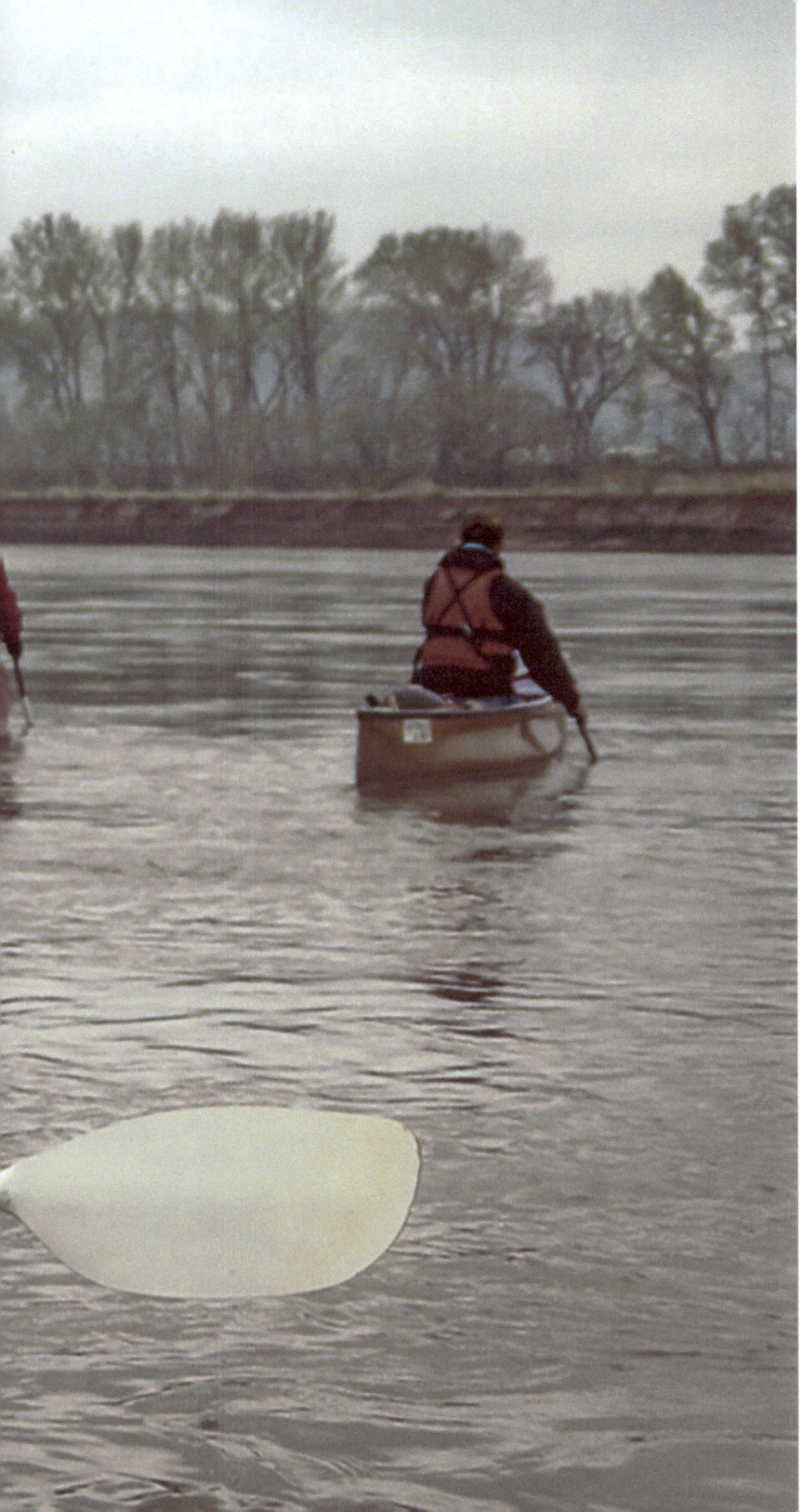

"AT MODERATE to low levels, the Kaw is one of America's best rivers for multi-day long-range wilderness style canoe and kayak tripping. I would say the upper third of the Kaw is the most beautiful section for doing such long trips, due to the many channel meanders and surrounding Flint Hills scenery."

- Joe Hyde

Tripping through the Flint Hills
Segment 25, Pottawatomie County

"WHY DO I LOVE THE KAW? I love the wildlife that makes their home on it, in it and along its shores. I love the mighty cottonwoods that grace its banks. I love the sand bars and the quiet to be found when floating on the river."

- Carey Maynard-Moody

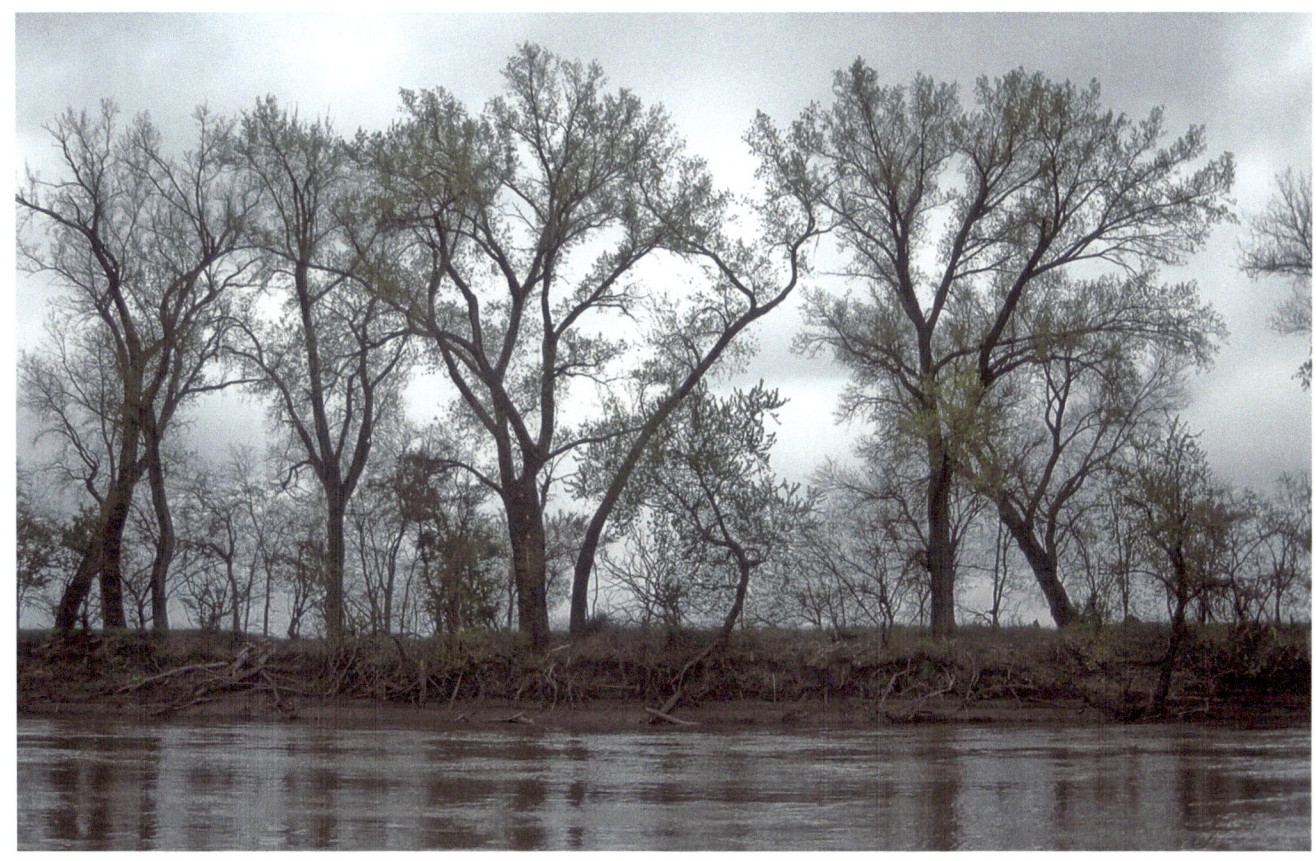

Cottonwoods in early spring
Segment 25, Riley County

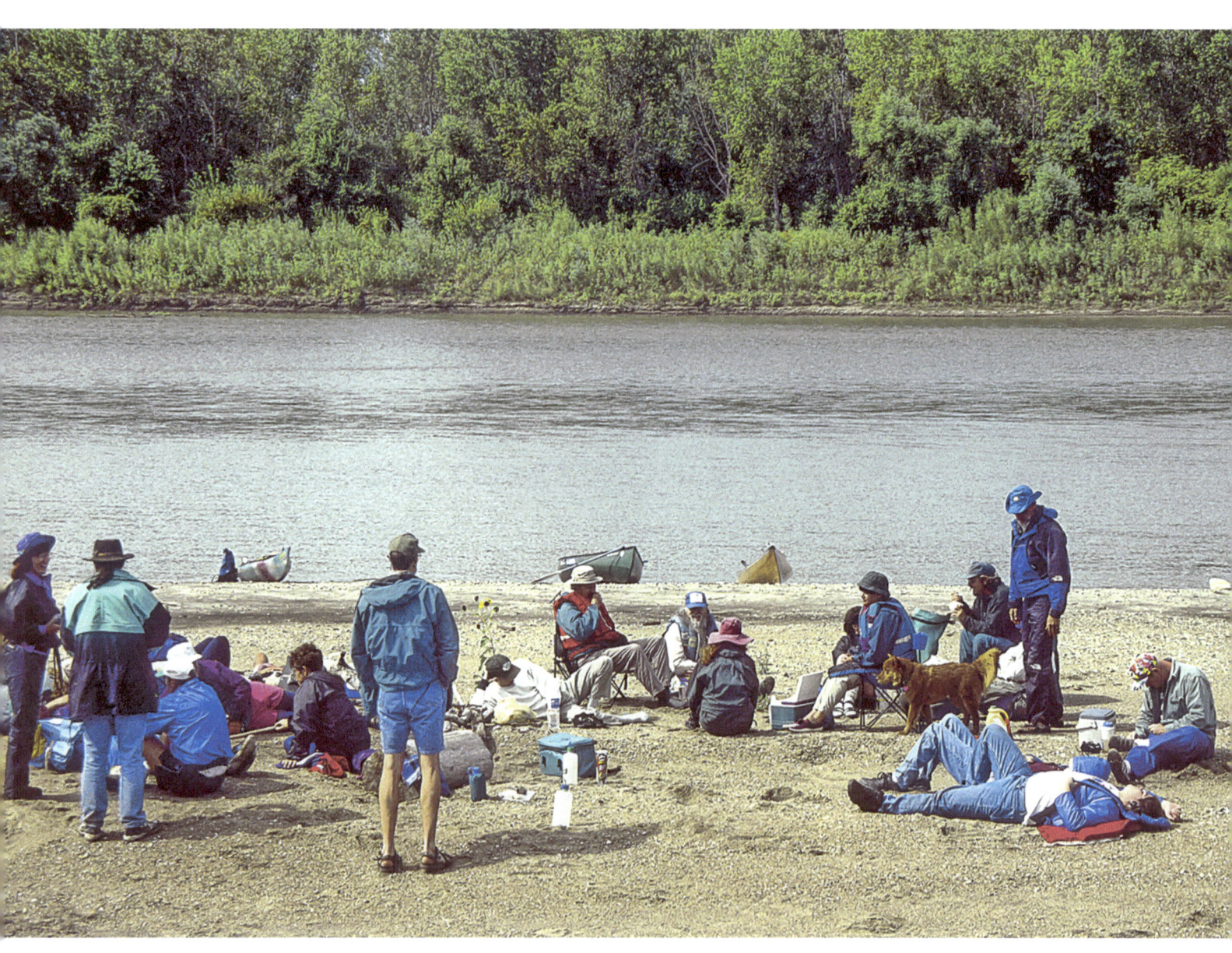

Sandbar picnic
Segment 25, Pottawatomie County

"ONE OF the most outstanding features of the Kaw are the many sand bars that can be used for picnics and camping."

\- Laura Calwell

"FLOATING THE KAW is a spiritual experience for me - the wildlife, the skies, the trees and the flowing water. What a wonderful sense that the universe is as it should be! It creates an inner peace that's hard to describe."

- Marilynn Koelliker

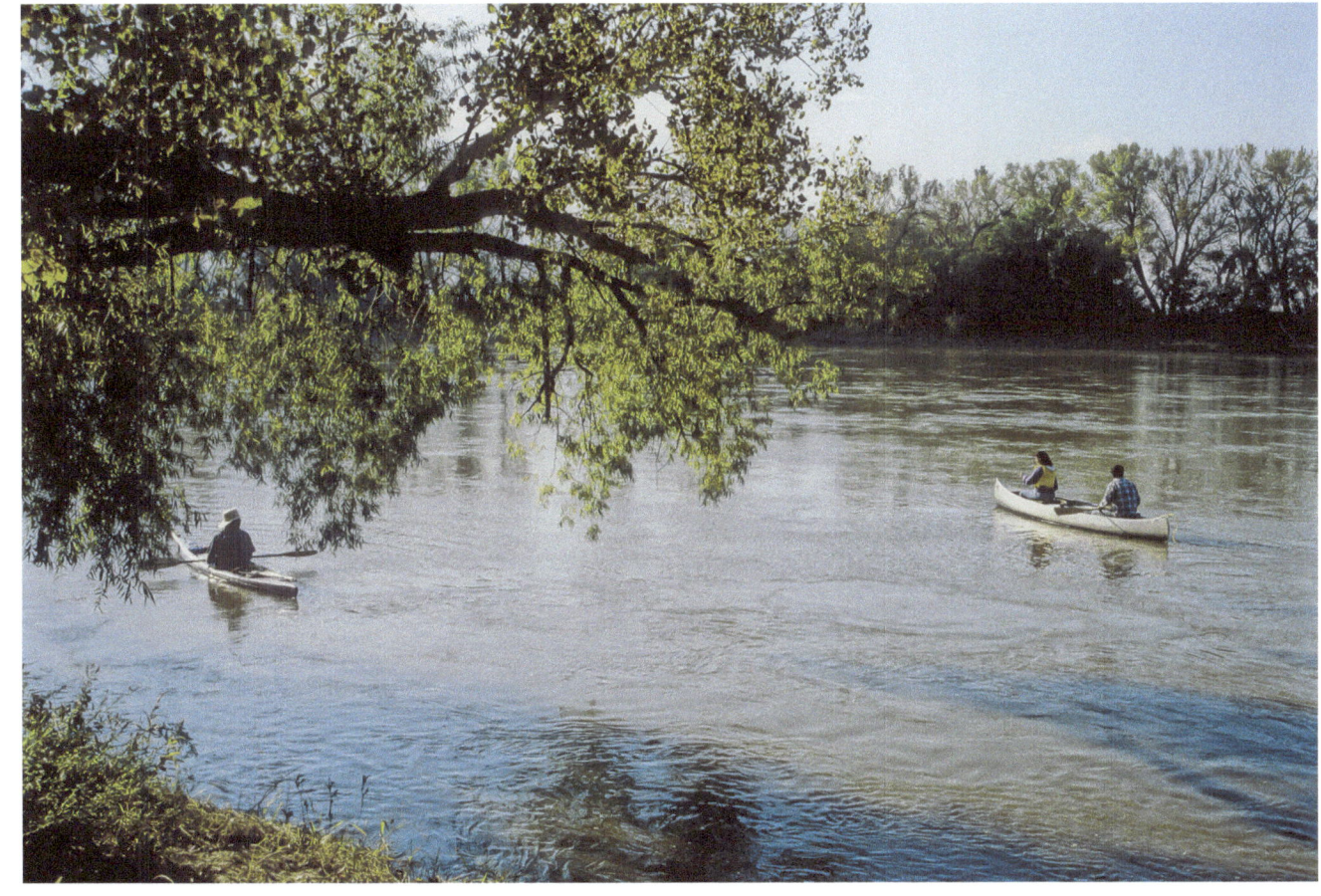

Early morning float near St. George
Segment 25, Pottawatomie County

46

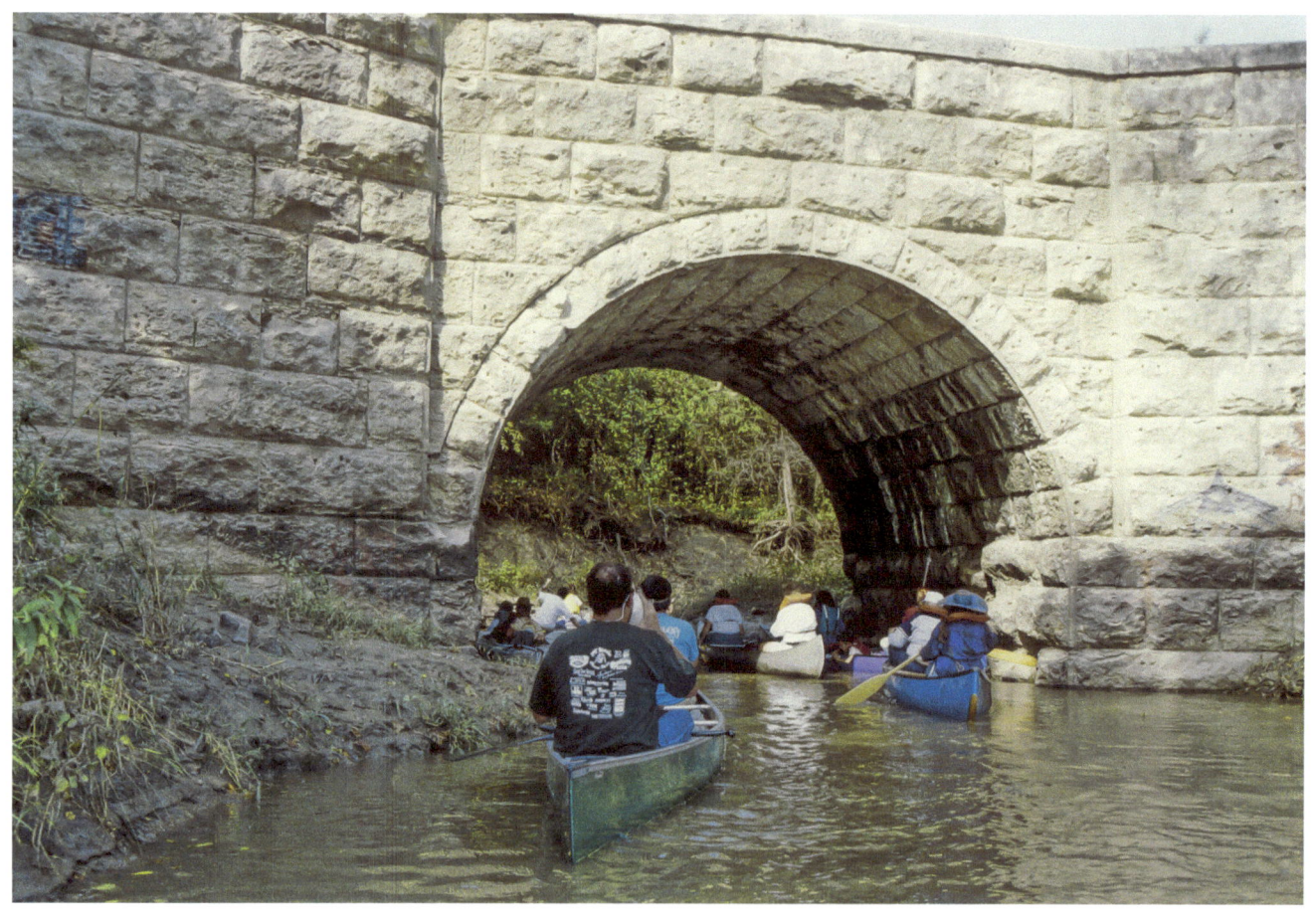

Exploring old stone train bridge
Segment 24, Pottawatomie County

"EVEN ON STRETCHES of the river I've paddled many times, I always discover some thing new."

- Bill Cutler

(overleaf)
Flint Hills scene near Wamego
Segment 24, Wabaunsee County

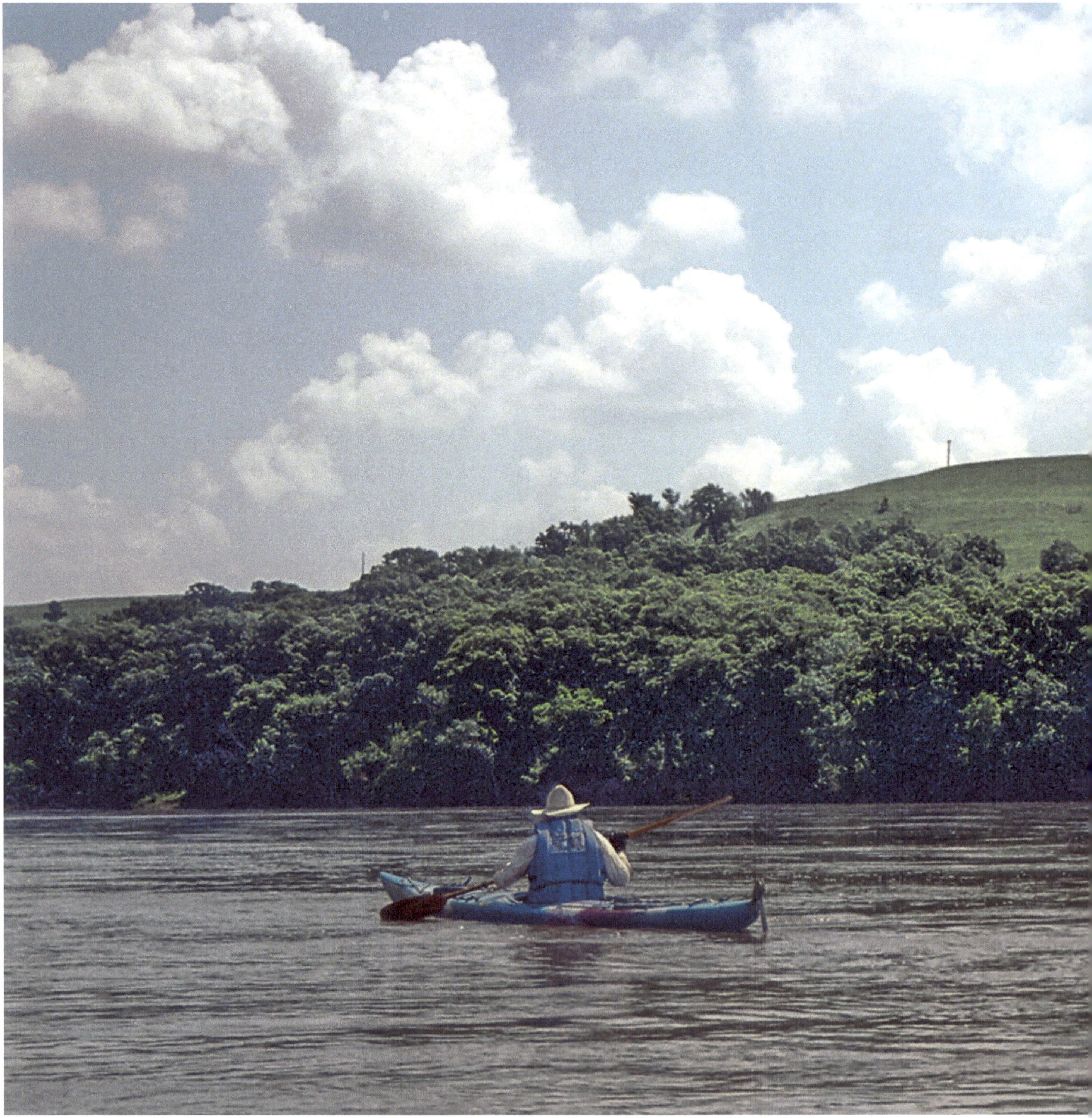

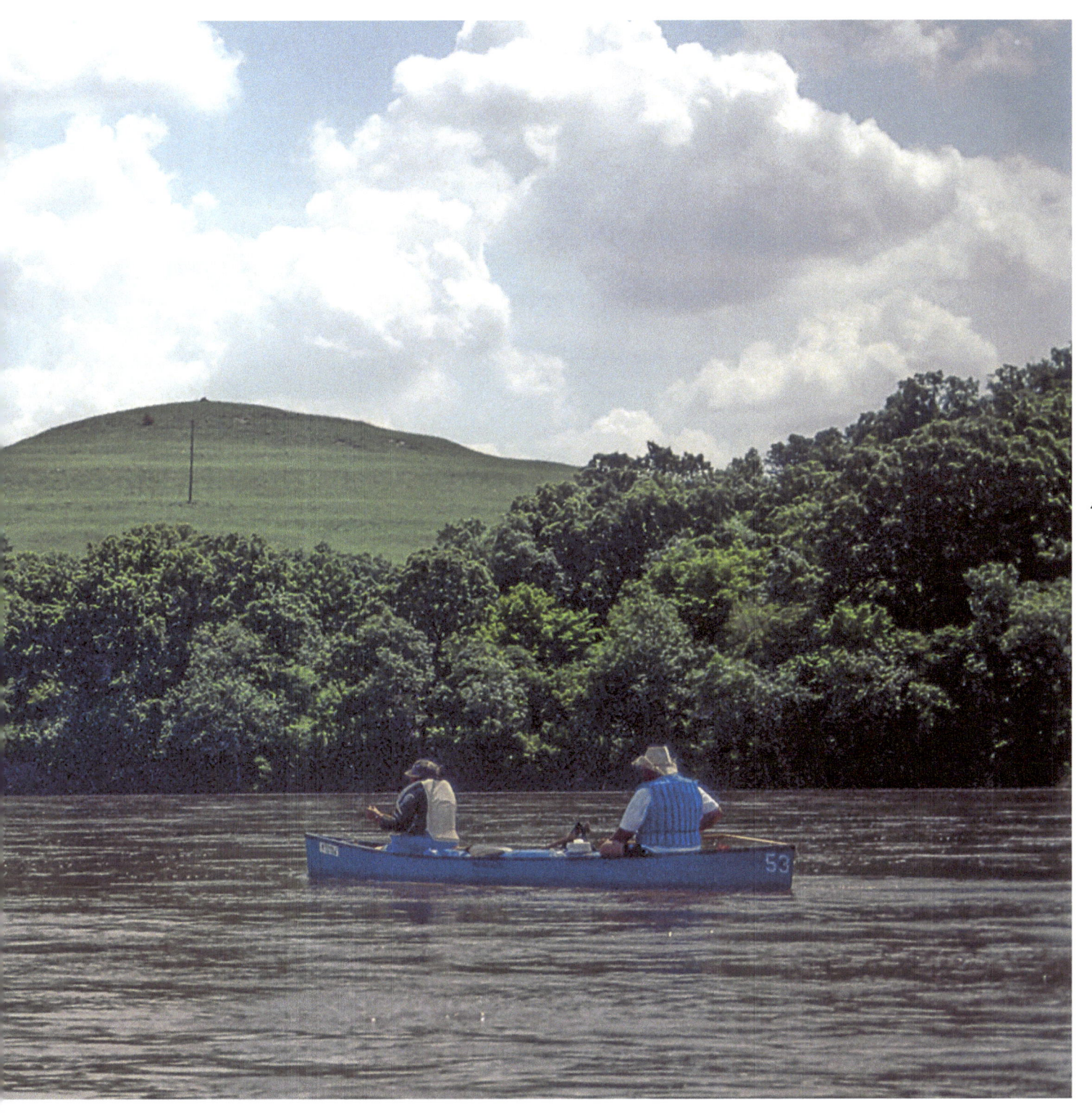

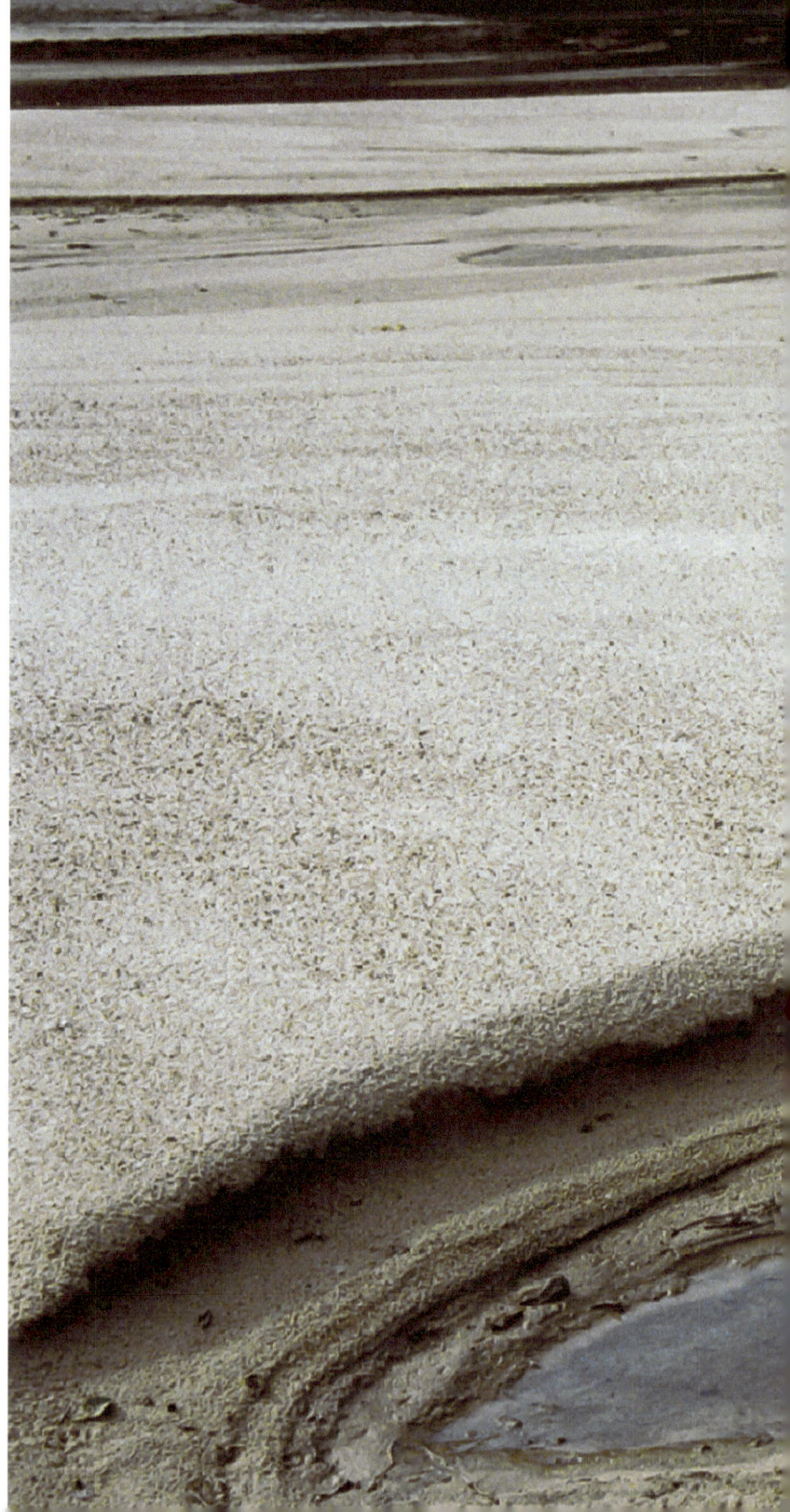

"I STAND on a sand bar sculptured by wind and water. I watch a red-tailed hawk soar on thermals overhead. From the branch of a dead tree, a turkey vulture watches me. Sunshine glistens on the surface of the water as I shove off to float down the Kaw River.**"**

-Rolland Love

50

Kaw sand bar
Segment 24, Pottawatomie County

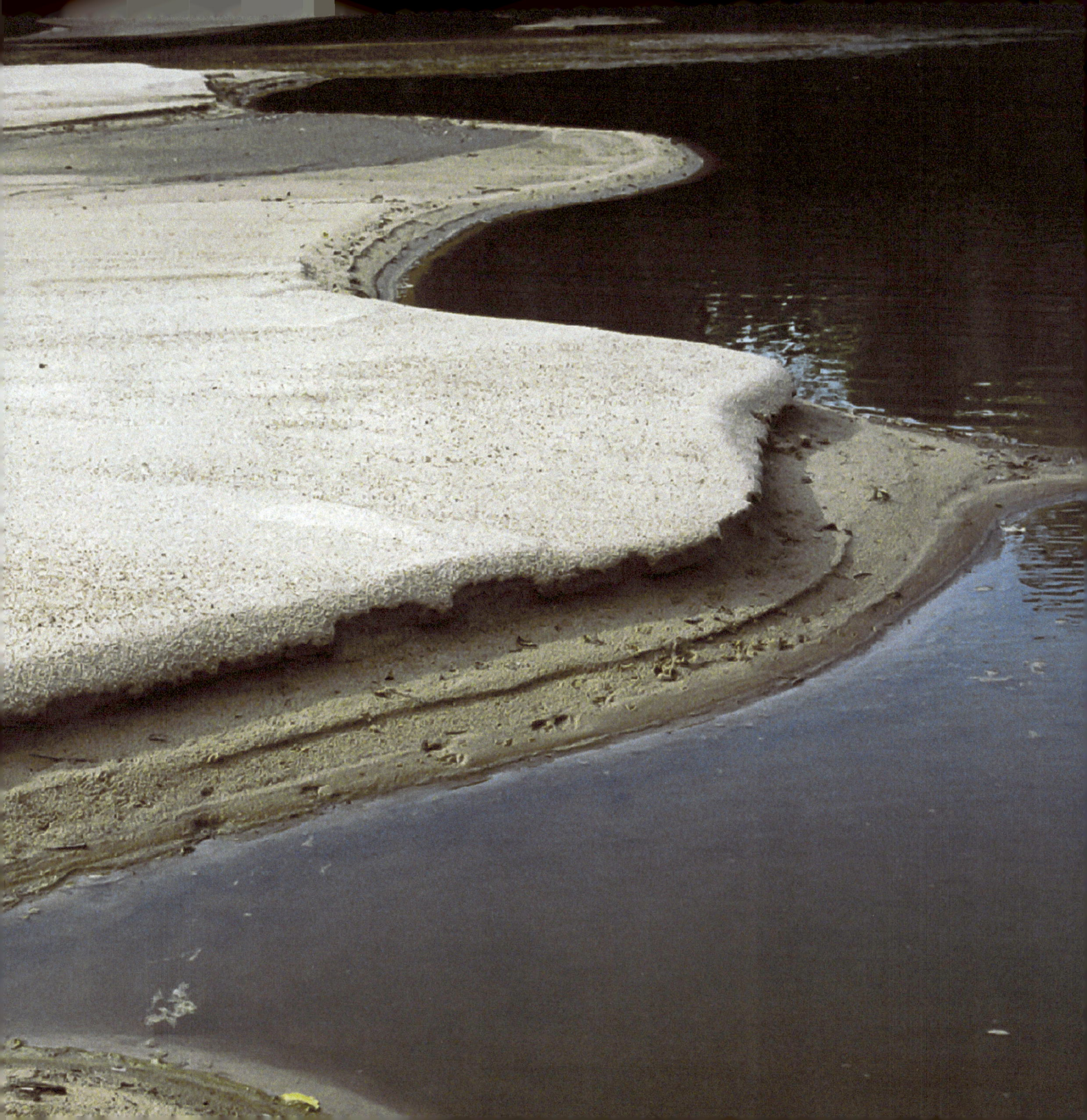

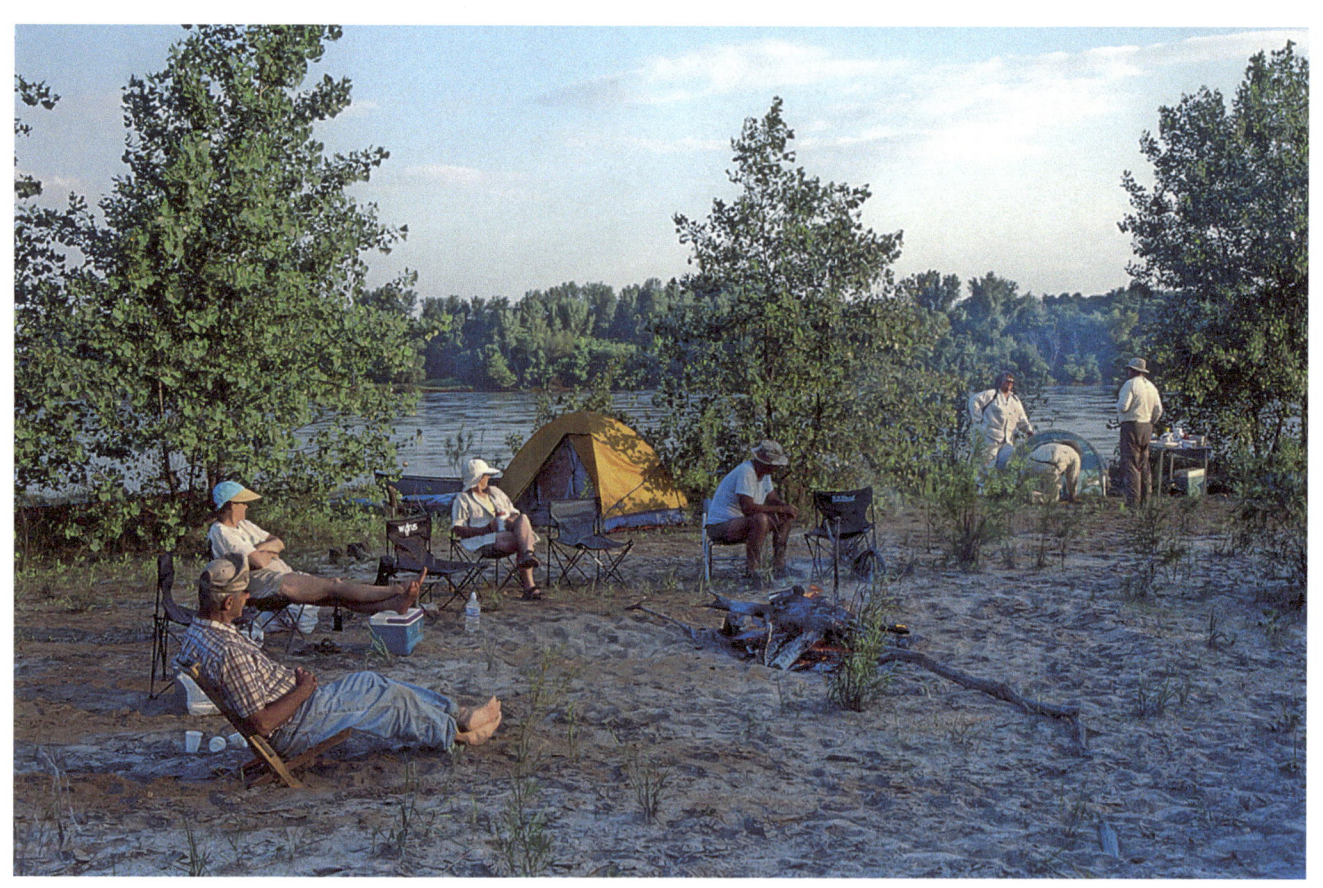

Campsite near Belvue
Segment 14, Pottawatomie County

"OUR FIRST CANOE TRIP down the Kaw River was in 1976. Since that time family and friends have always spent two and a half days, Memorial Day weekend, canoeing rivers and camping on sand bars; many times on the Kansas River. The quality of this experience is one of the best kept secrets in Kansas."

- David J. Karnowski

"WHEN YOU SPEND a long day on the Kaw soaking up sun all the while retracing imagined sandy footprints from past trips you have experienced, you possess a comfortable familiarity to something that you know is in constant flux. But it feels so steady, reliable and unchanging on those warm afternoons. You forget the Kaw is wild. You set up camp and instinctively look west, waiting. And when the last sliver of vermilion streaked water rests in a place far from where you sit, the night approaches."

- Christina Ruiz

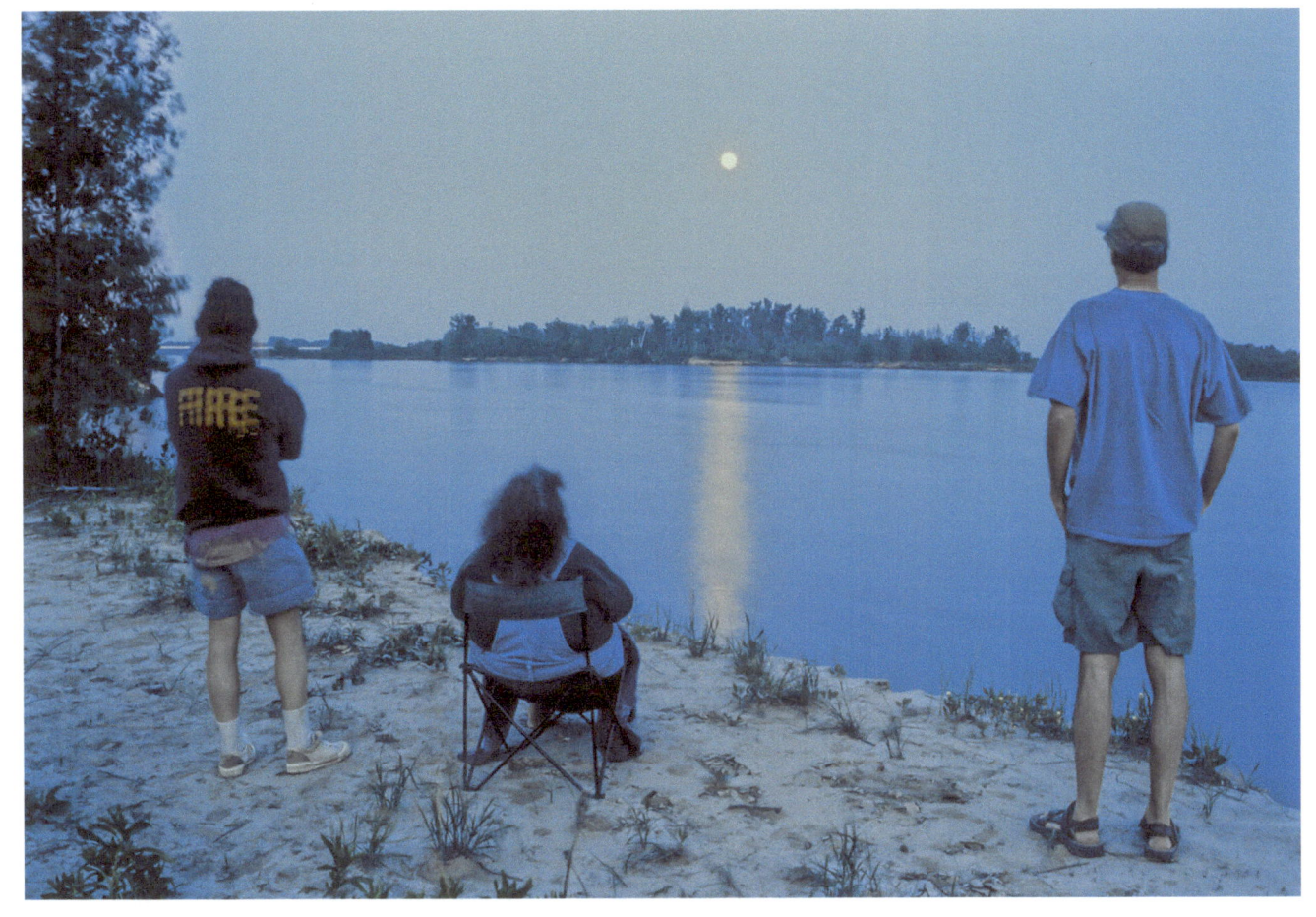

Moonglow on the Kaw
Segment 14, Pottawatomie County

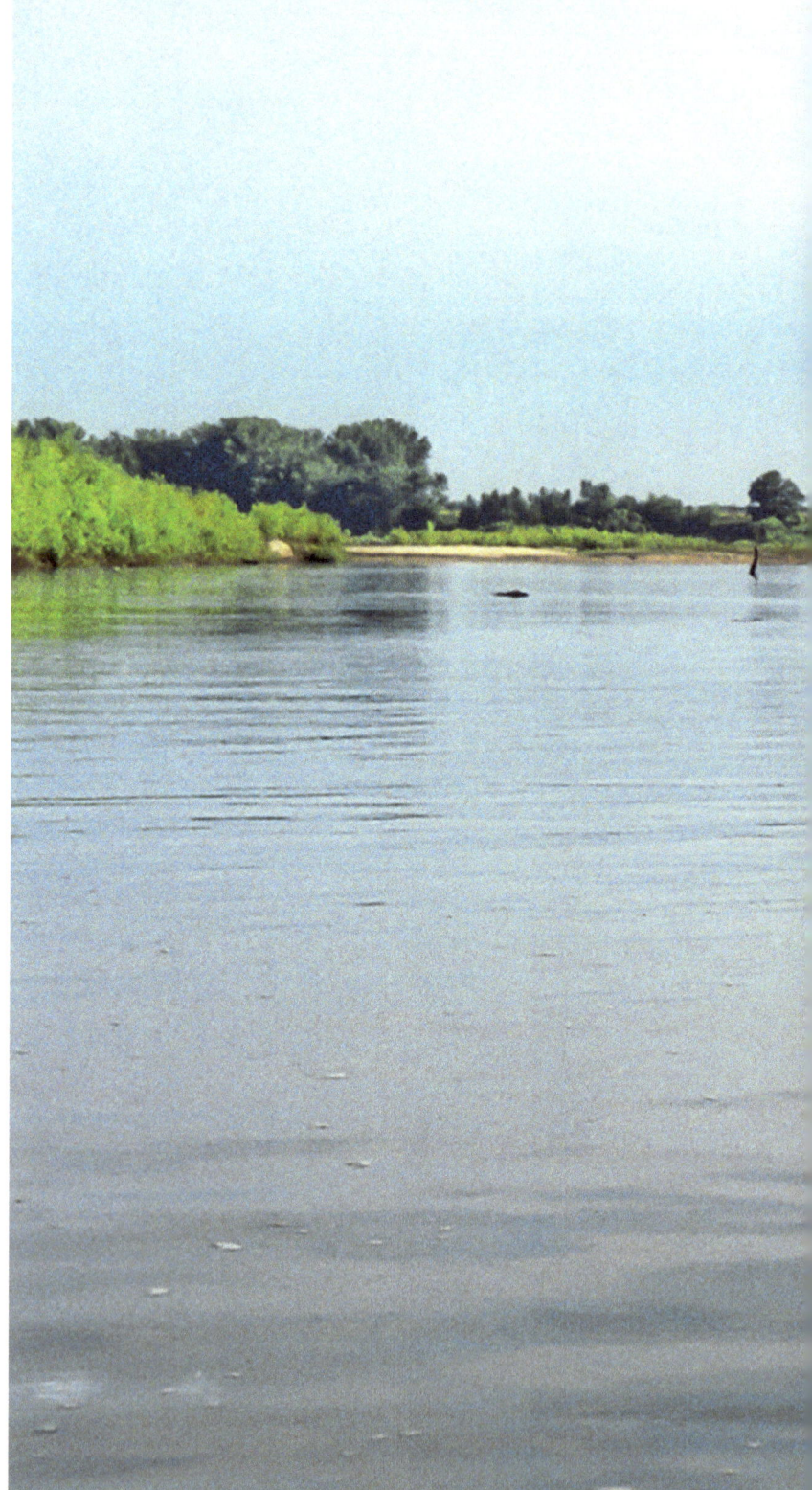

"A RIVER, like the Kaw, helps us to feel the rhythm of life. The Kaw is an ancient river and the lifeblood for much of Kansas."

- Tom Gallegos

56

Glacial rock island
Segment 14, Wabaunsee County

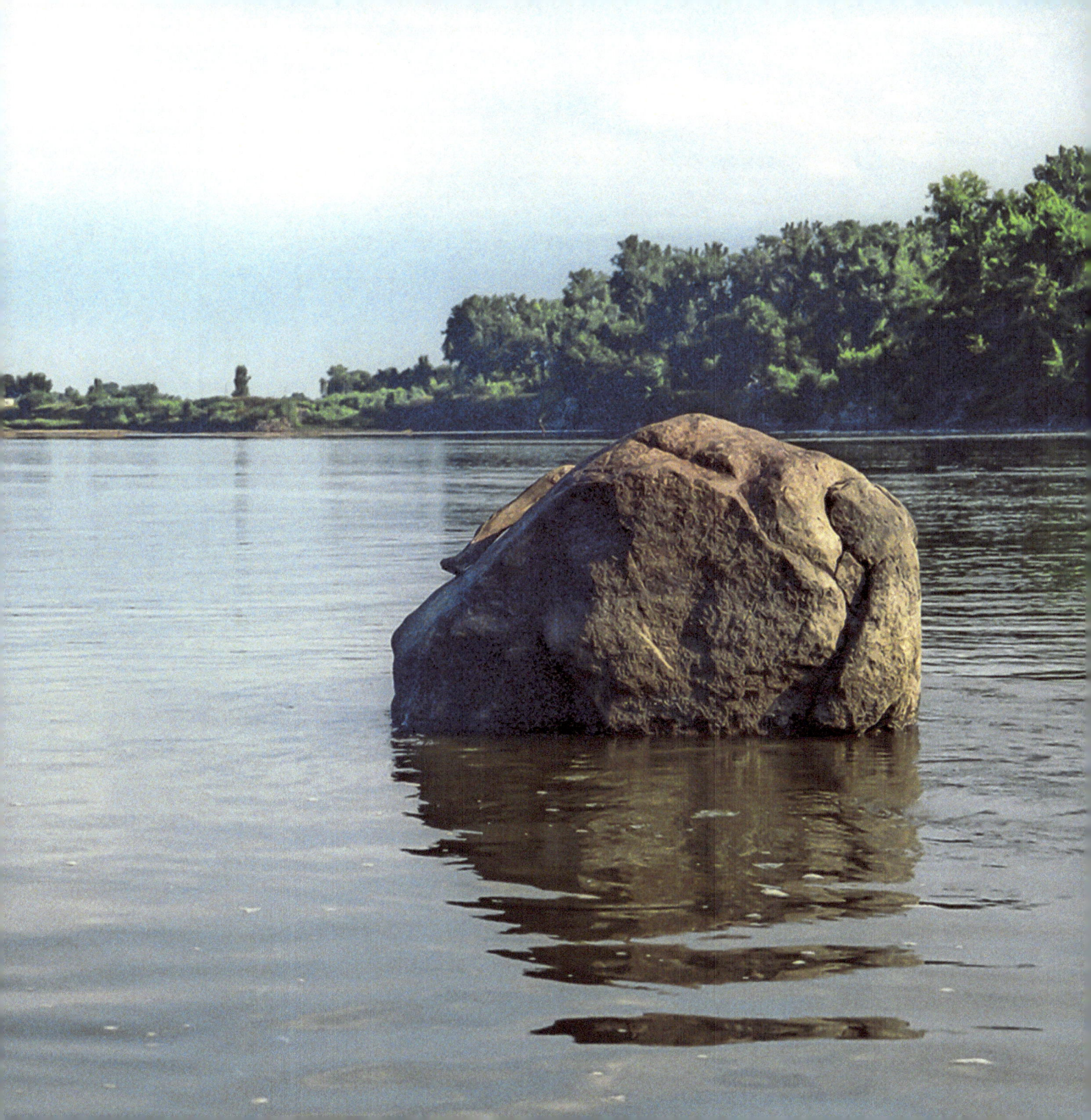

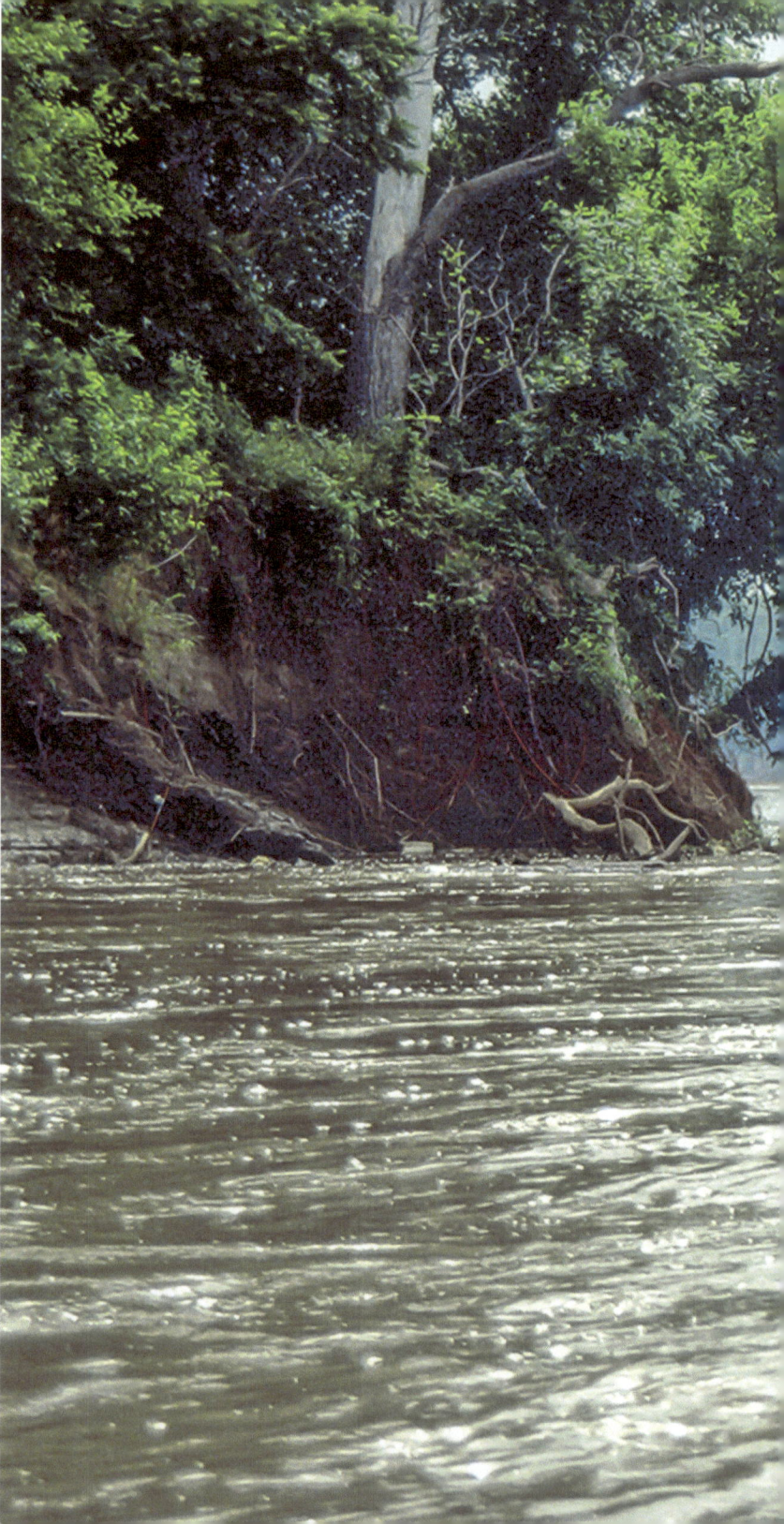

"HOW EASY
it is to feel isolated
while you're on the
river. Even though,
if you just climb up
the riverbank, you'll
find a major highway
or small town nearby.**"**

- Gary Ficklin

58

Paddling a swift current
Segment 13, Shawnee County

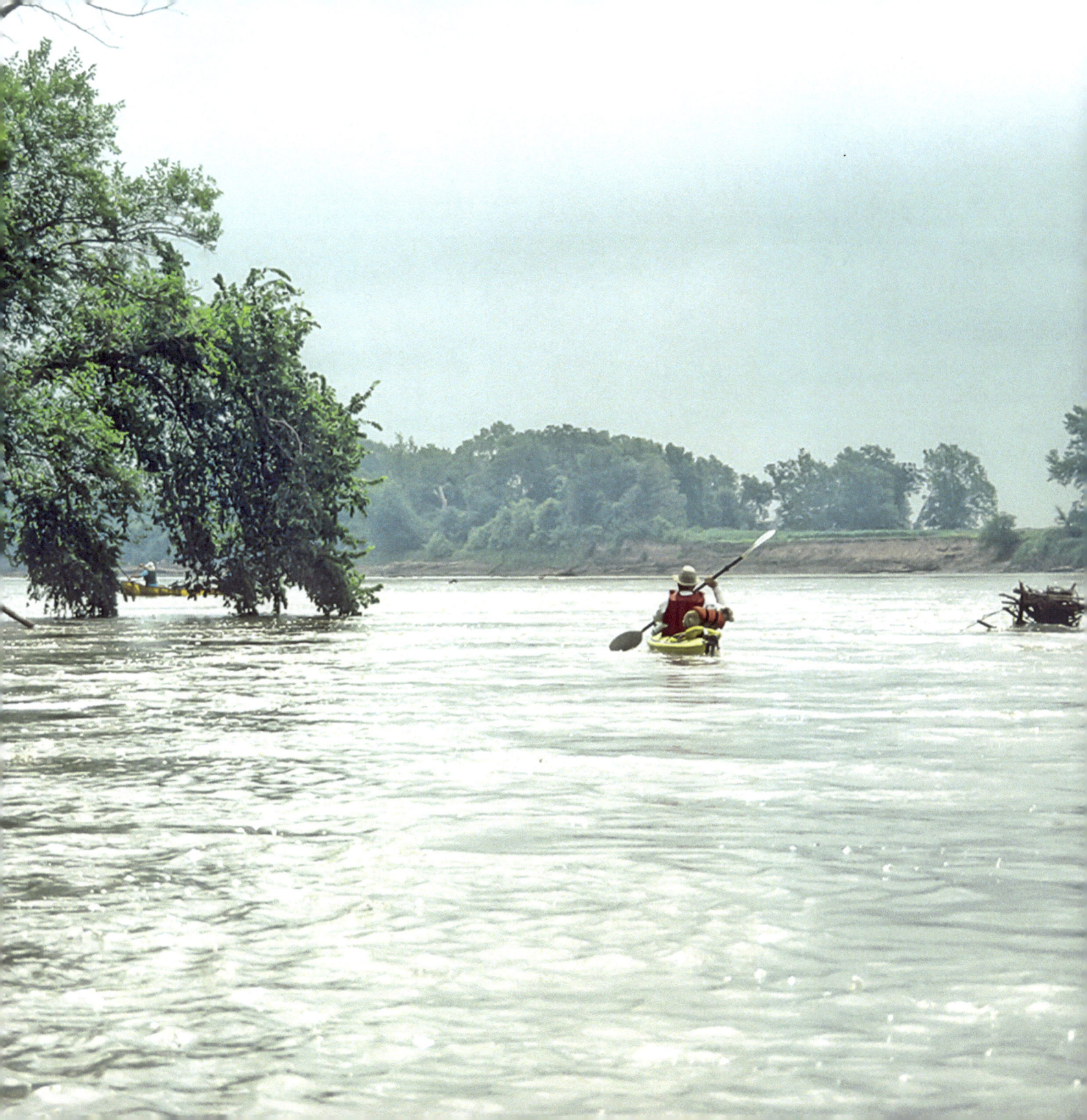

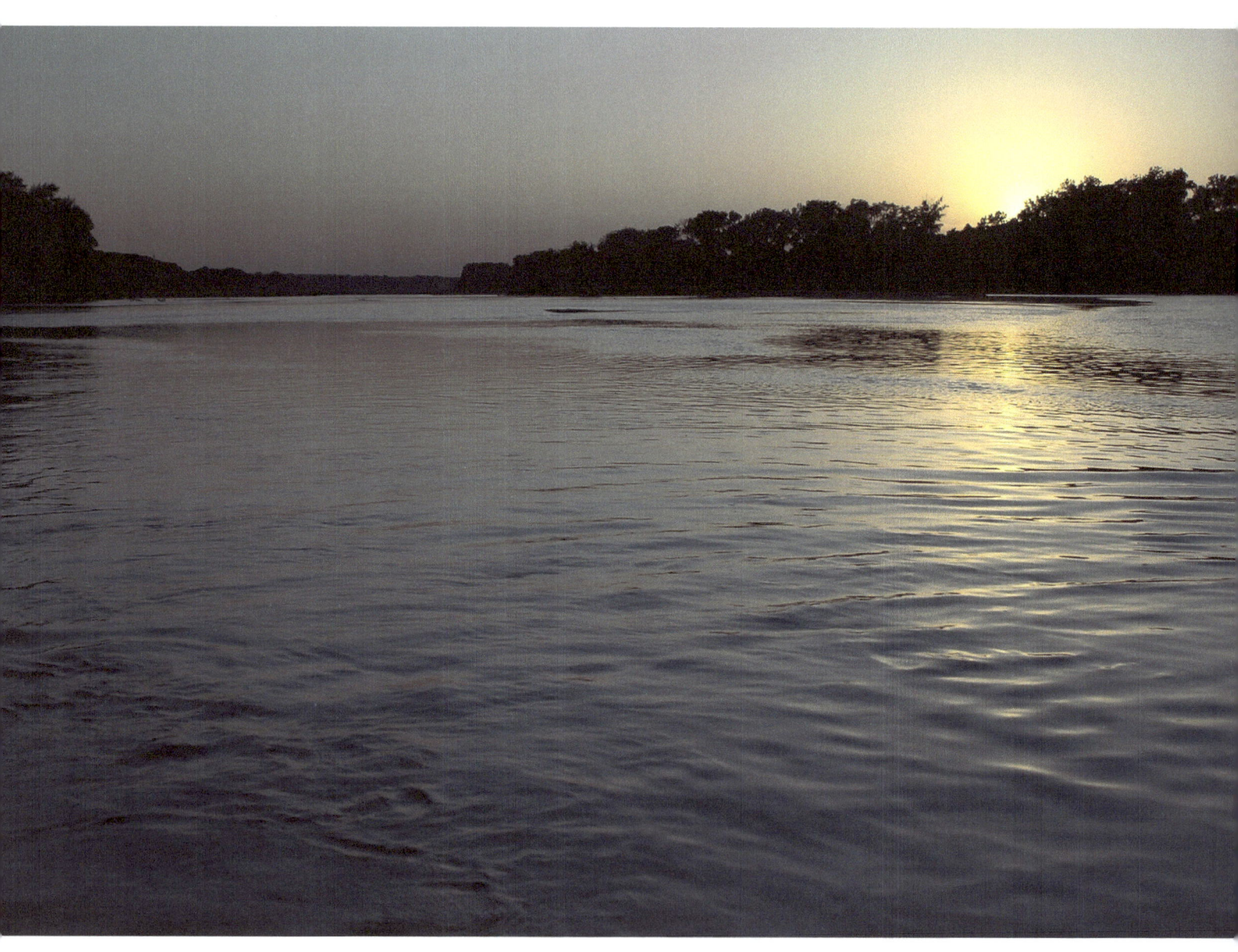

Kaw in twilight
Segment 11, Shawnee County

"FROM THE SMALLEST RIPPLES on the surface can be read the movement of air, the speed of current, the shape of riverbed, the depth of water, and where food is to be found. Each meander revealed a path, each sandbar a pattern. Every floating leaf, projecting twig and ripple communicated a wealth of information about the river's elusive ways. The Kaw, like and unlike any river, whispers secrets that few will hear and even fewer will understand."

- Dave Murphy

"THE KAW continues to invite anyone with a deep and abiding respect for nature to float its shallow waters and explore its shifting channels and ever-changing sandbars. This beautiful prairie stream offers truly outstanding recreational opportunities."

- Bob Angelo

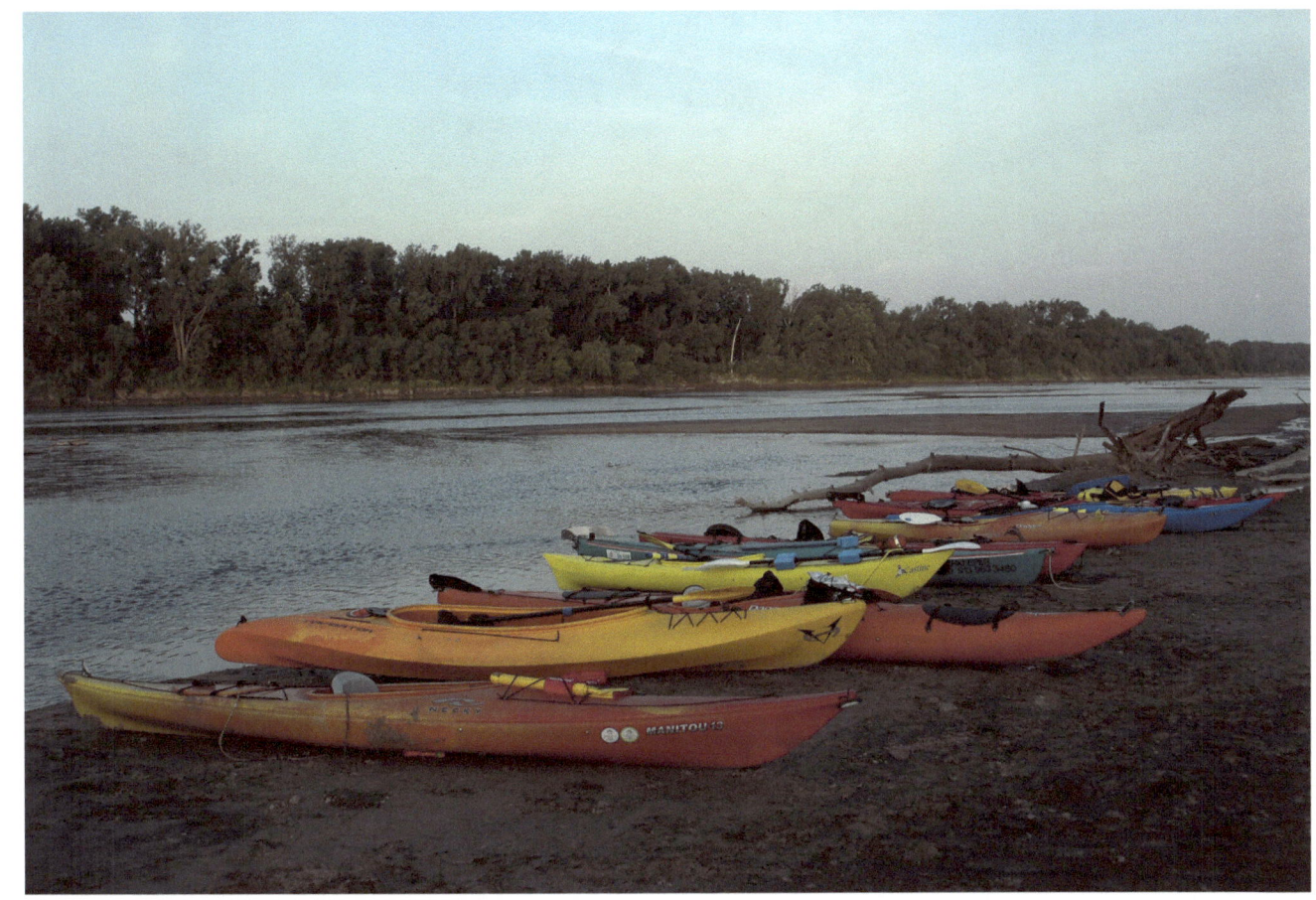

Kayaks parked on sandbar
Segment 11, Shawnee County

"AFTER CAMPING out on the river that night, we woke to find everything shrouded in a thick blanket of fog. We glided out into the mist, slicing through it as the sun slowly shone through and finally burned it all away.**"**

— Patty Boyer

65

Sunrise at Kaw River State Park
Segment 10, Shawnee County

Bald Eagle soaring
Segment 10, Shawnee County

"THE QUALITY of my life is enhanced when I float quietly down the river while watching an eagle glide high overhead."

- R. J. Stephenson

(overleaf)
Heron tracks in sandbar
Segment 10, Shawnee County

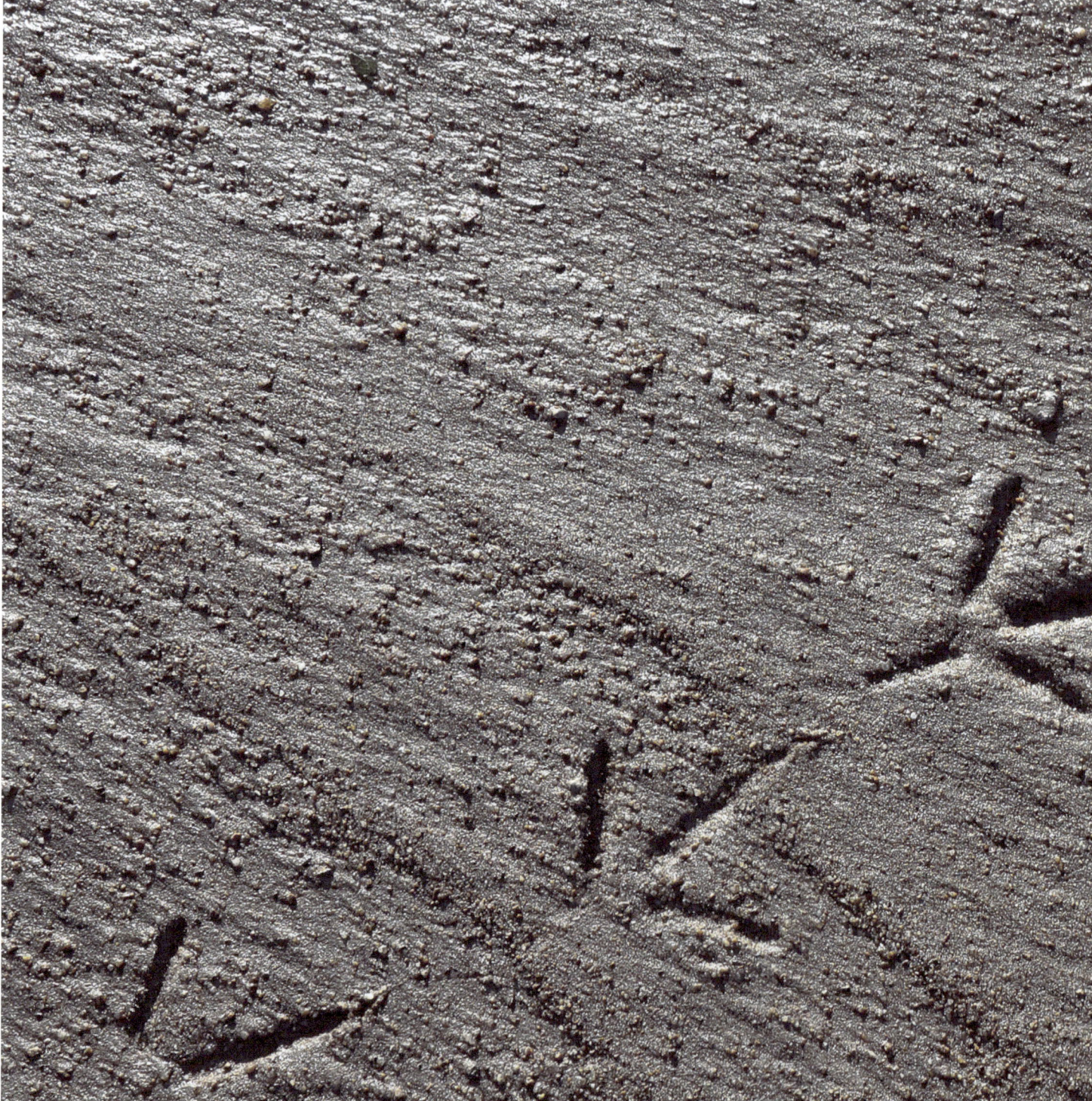

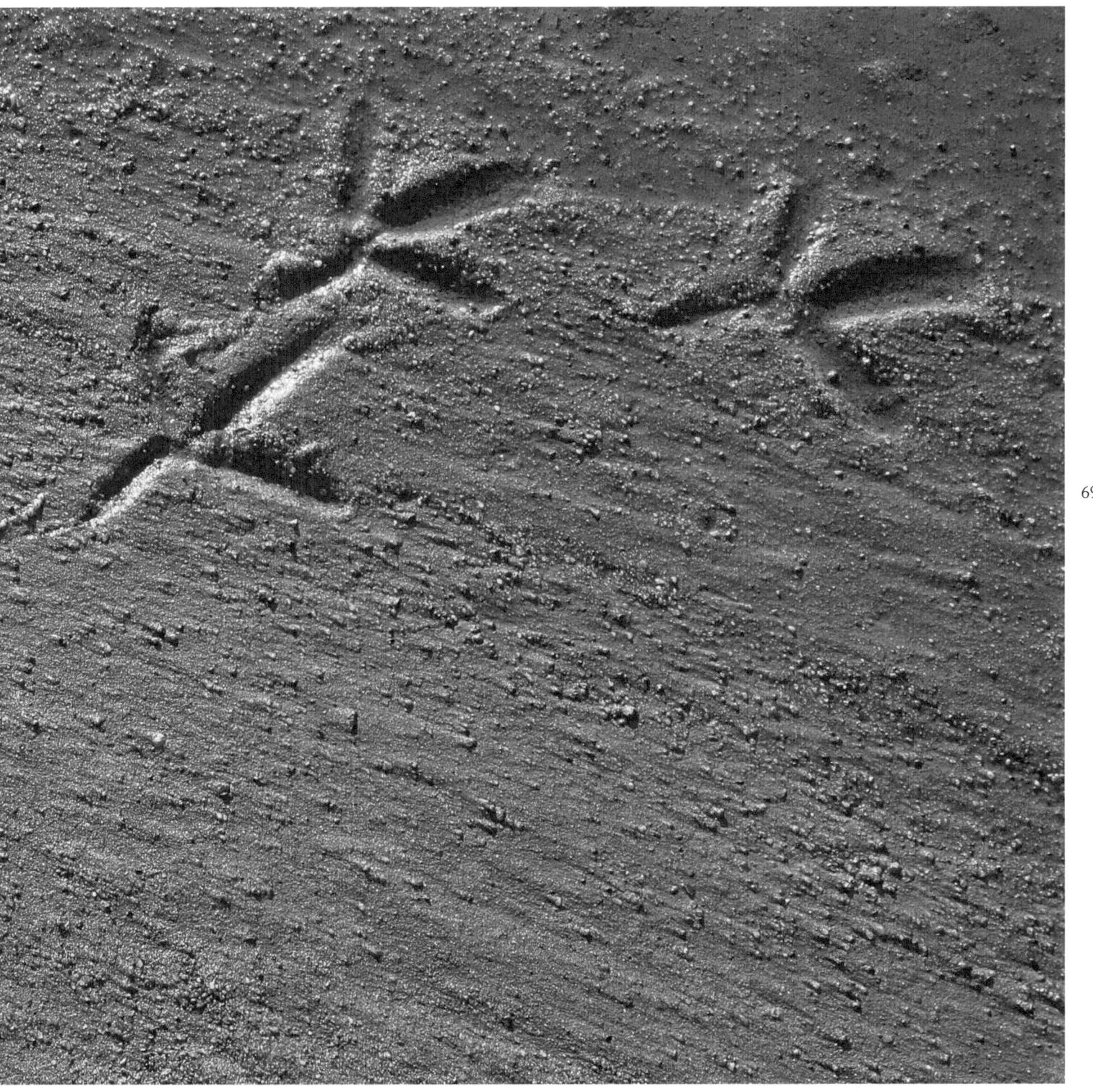

Buttonbush and butterfly
Segment 10, Shawnee County

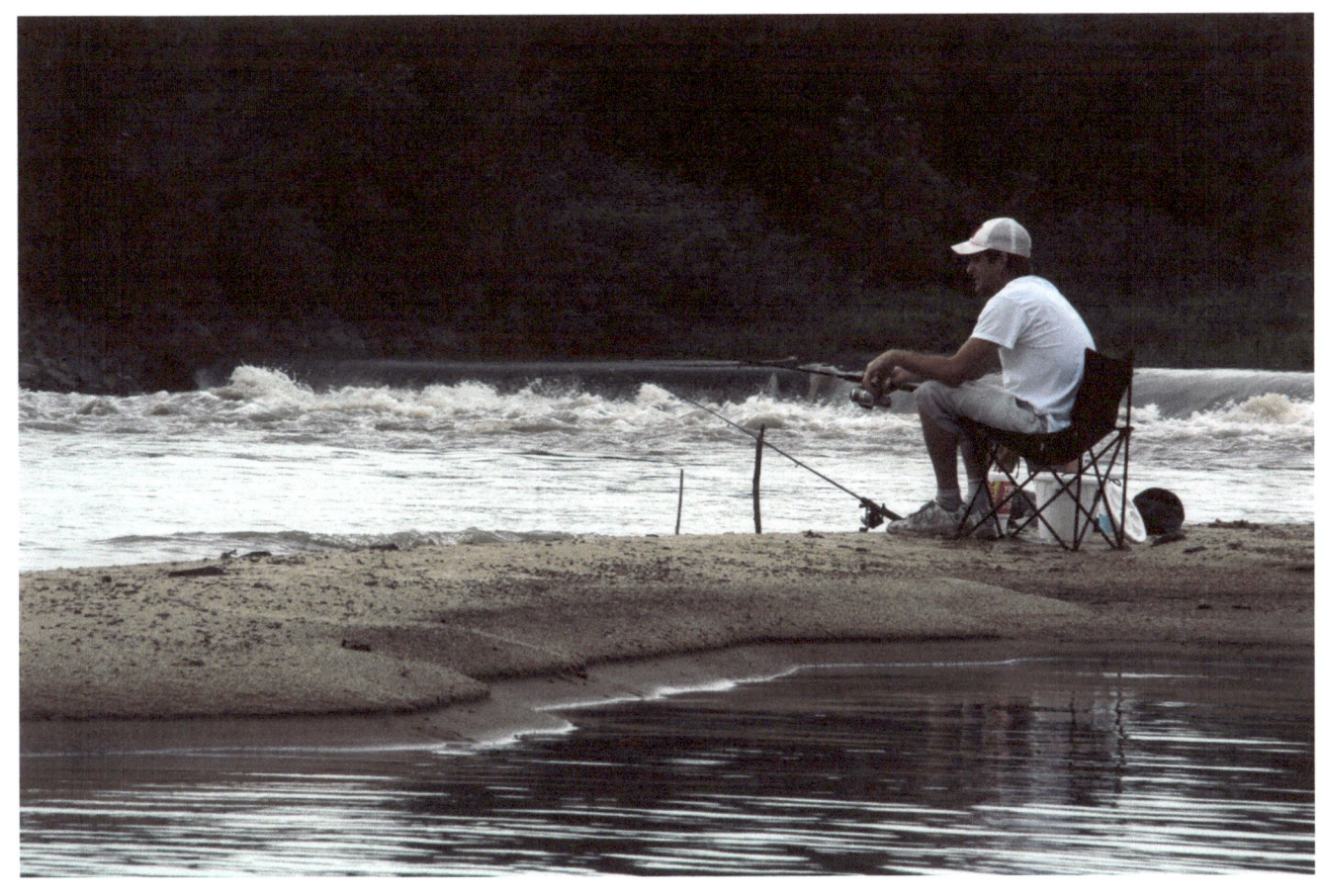

Fishing near the Topeka weir
Segment 10, Shawnee County

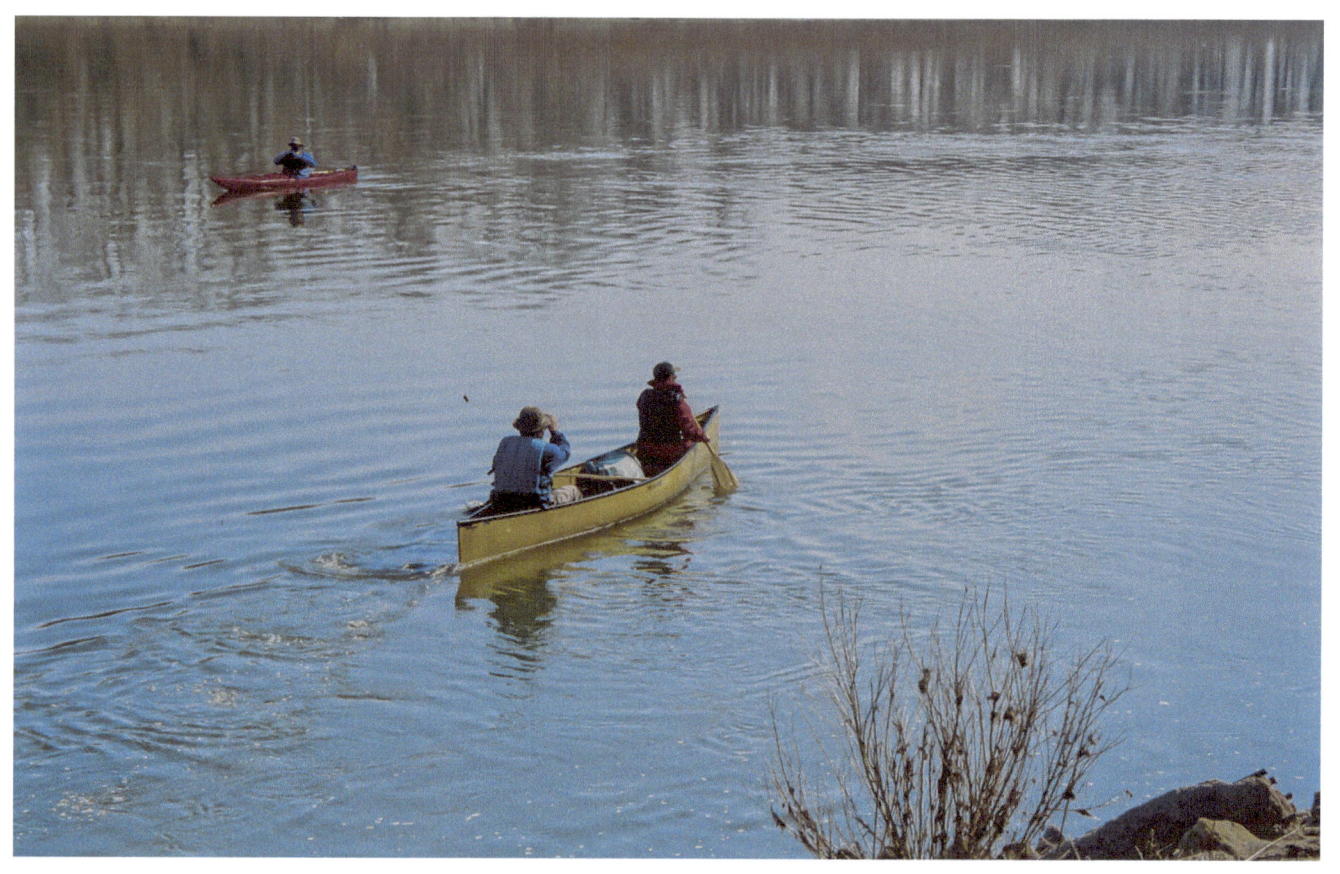

Quietly exploring the Kaw
Segment 4, Shawnee County

"AN OZARK STREAM, it's not. The Kaw's lack of clarity and speed of flow, however, is offset by the solitude afforded within minutes, not hours of home. Most importantly, it's ours to be protected, enhanced and enjoyed."

- Hank Ernst

"THANKS to Friends of the Kaw, and the support of former Governor Mike Hayden, we're seeing a growing number of access points that make it easy to get on the water, and have a place to leave your car. It sure beats dragging your boat through the weeds and poison ivy and wondering if you'll get a ticket for leaving your car along the road."

        - Bill Cutler

74

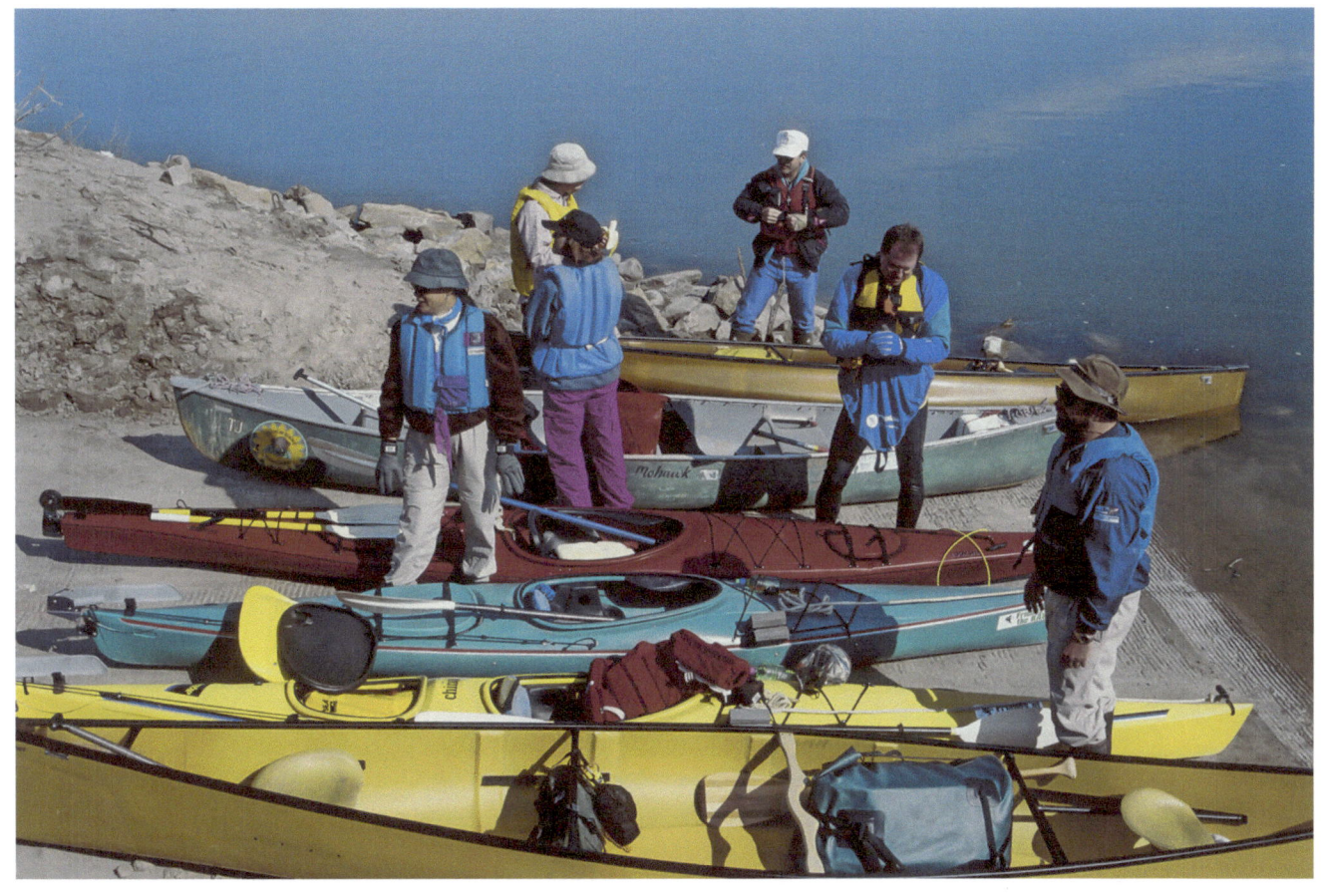

Preparing for the launch
Segment 4, Shawnee County

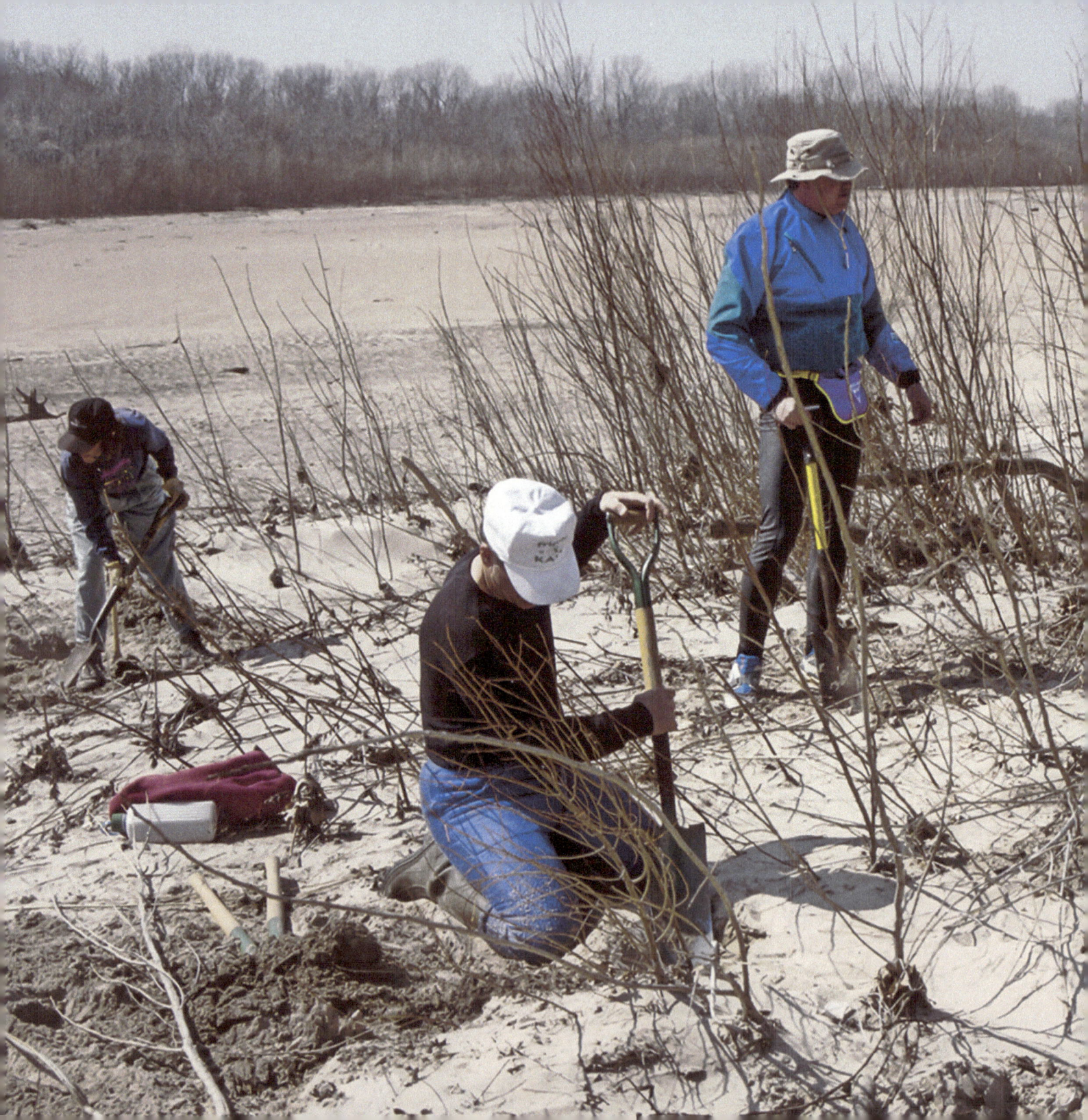

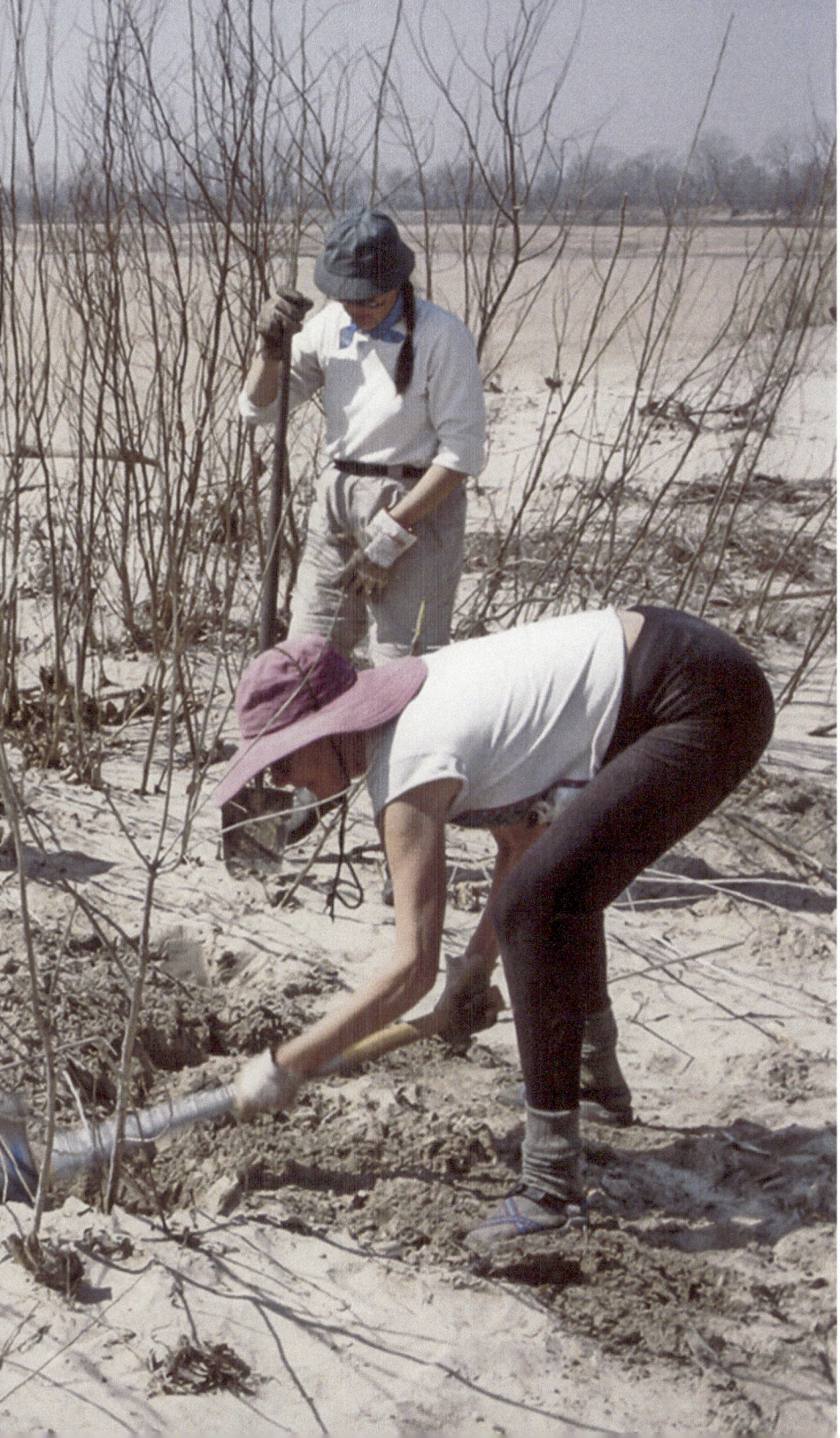

"**THE KAW** brings together people with a common sense of adventure, and a reverence for the natural world."

- Chip Farley

Least Tern habitat restoration
Segment 3, Shawnee County

"LIKE A MIRROR opens up a room and expands the space so does the flat water. It doubles the sky.**"**

– Lisa Grossman

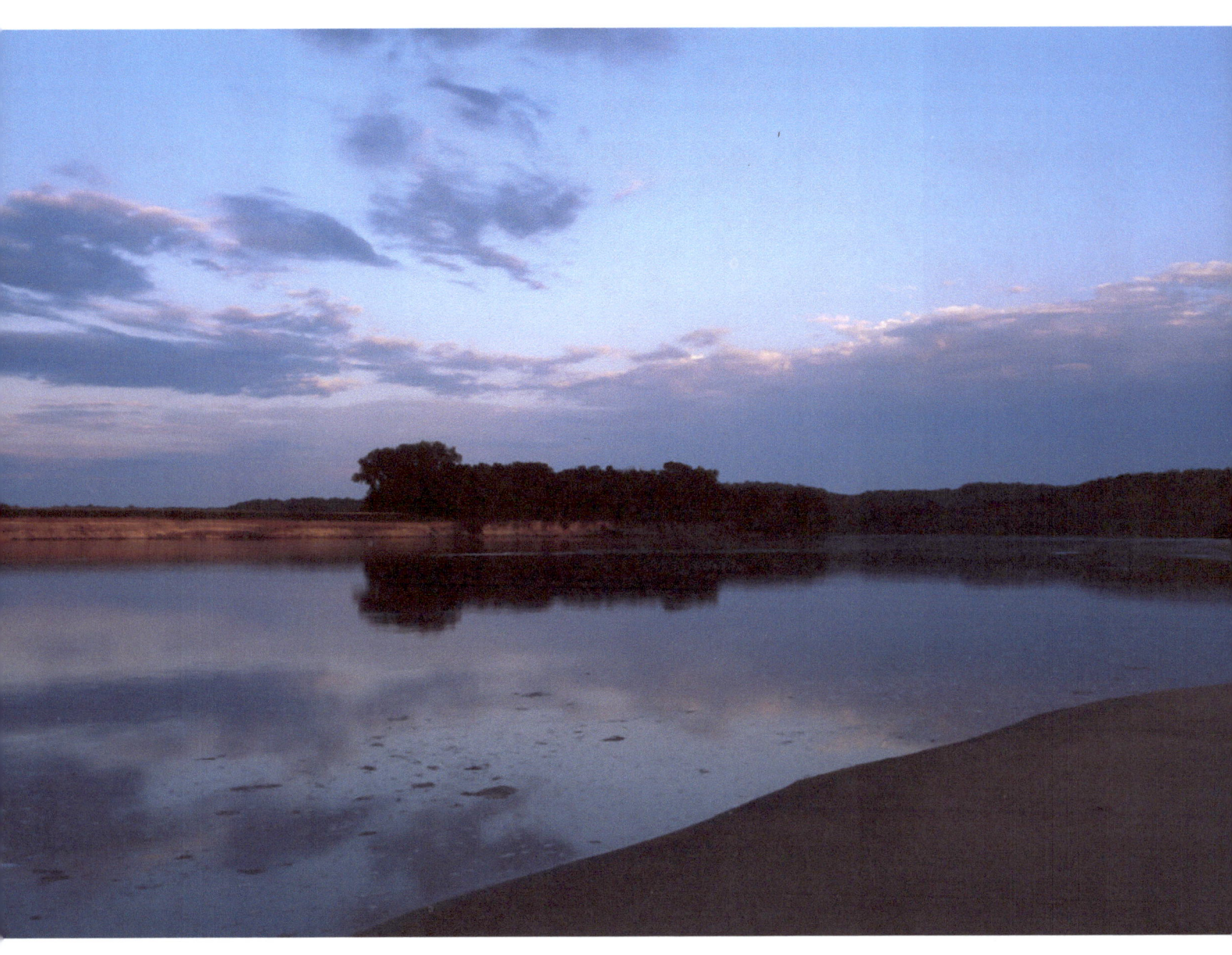

Afternoon glow on the Kaw
Segment 1, Jefferson County

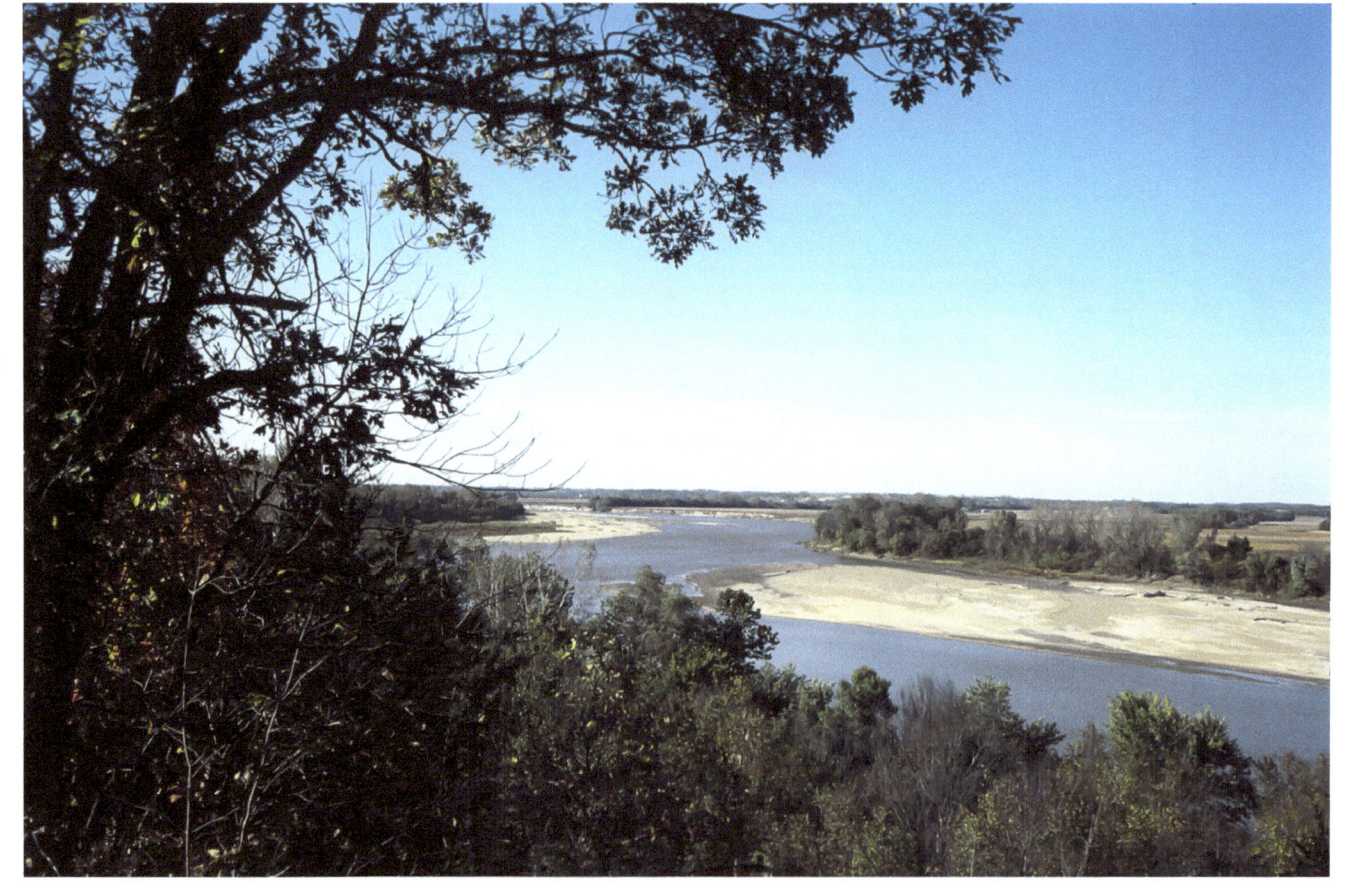

Overlook on scenic river road
Segment 1, Douglas County

"THE RIVER FLOWS ON, curving through history, twisting through space, remembering and restoring, moving us."

— Elizabeth Schultz

"AS A CHILD my grandfather planted the fear of God in me concerning being on or near the Kaw river. So when I canoed down the Delaware river from the dam of Lake Perry toward the "treacherous" Kaw, I felt a tingle, remembering his warnings. As I entered the Kaw, along with numerous other paddlers, my fears evaporated into amazement to be floating for the first time the "forbidden" body of water. It seemed almost mystical - like floating on air."

- Charles H. Vausbinder

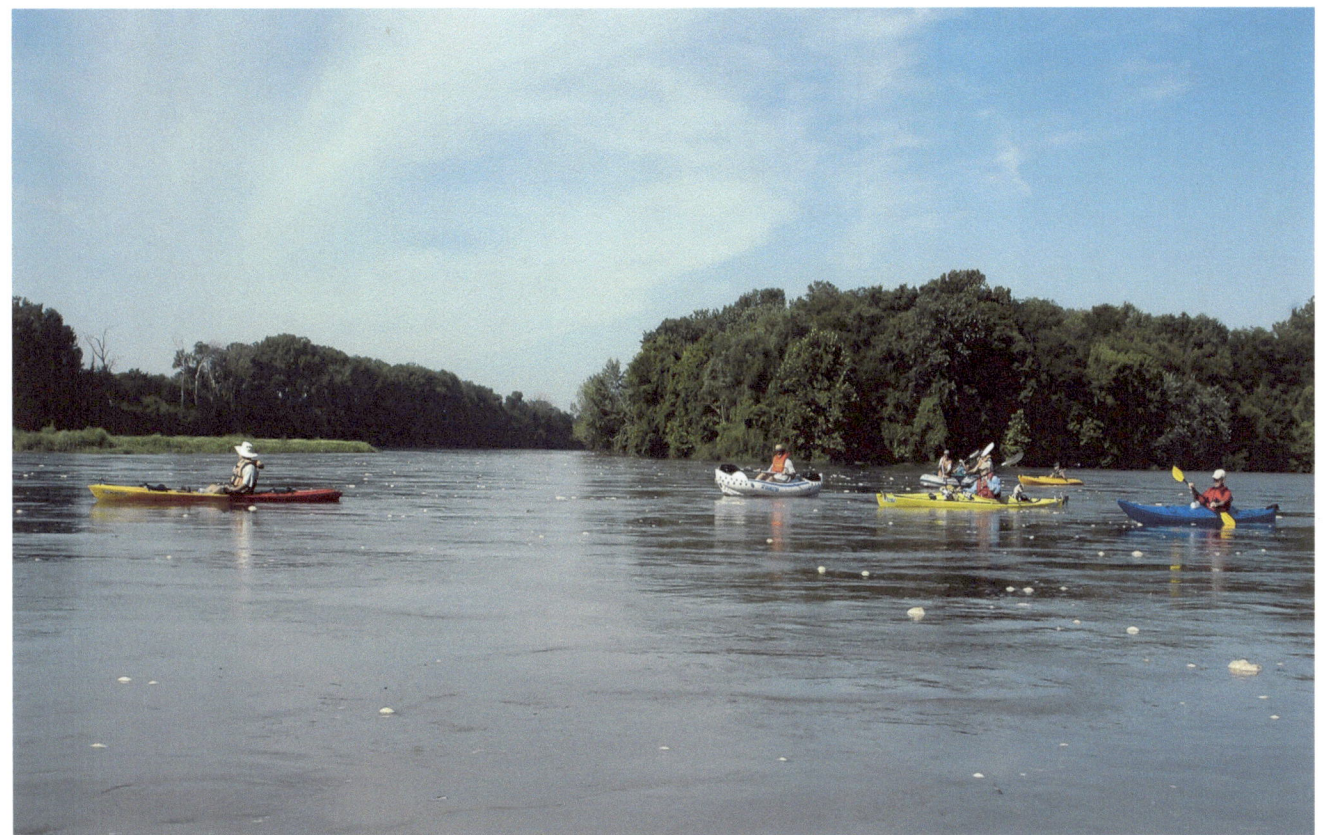

Floating into the big river
Segment 1, Jefferson County

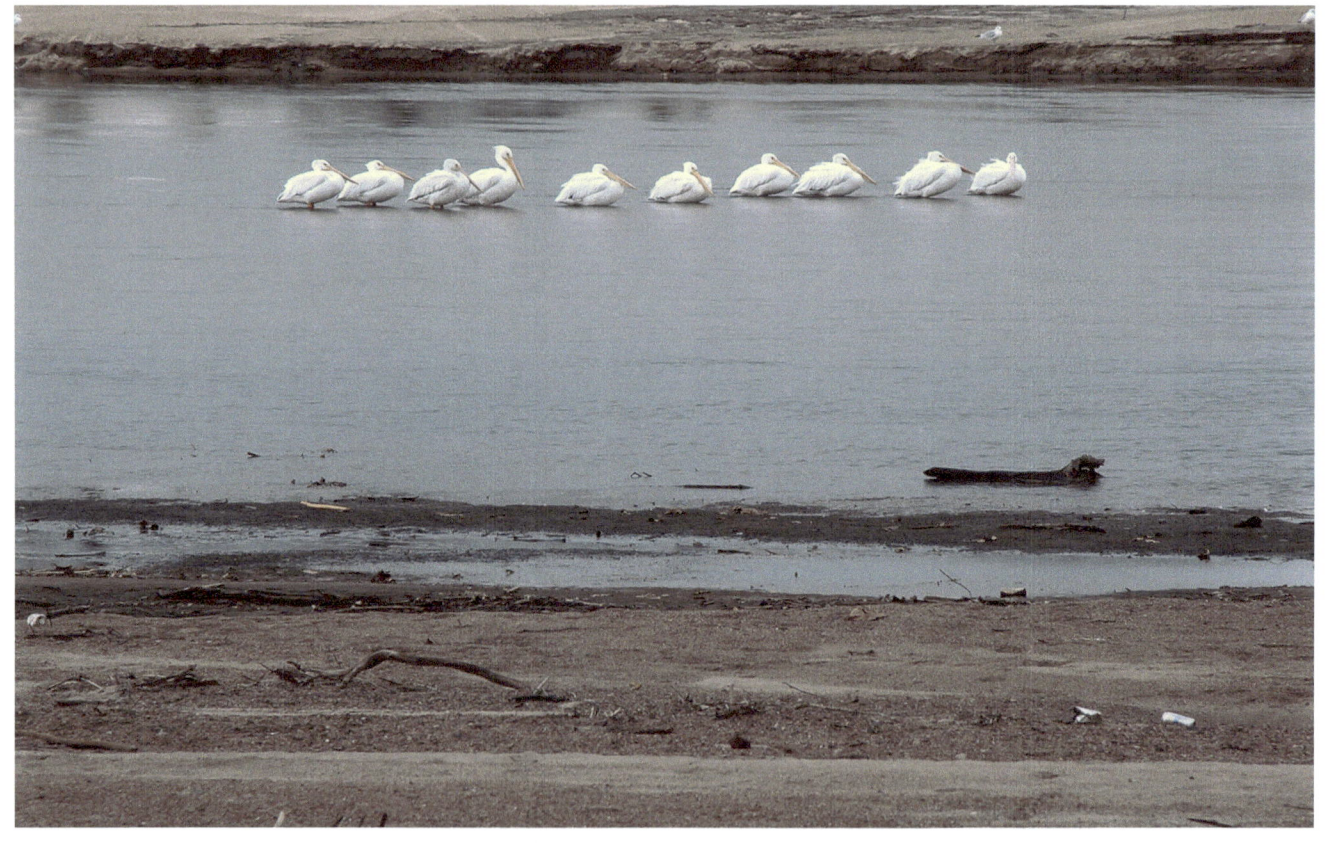

Pelicans resting in channel
Segment 1, Jefferson County

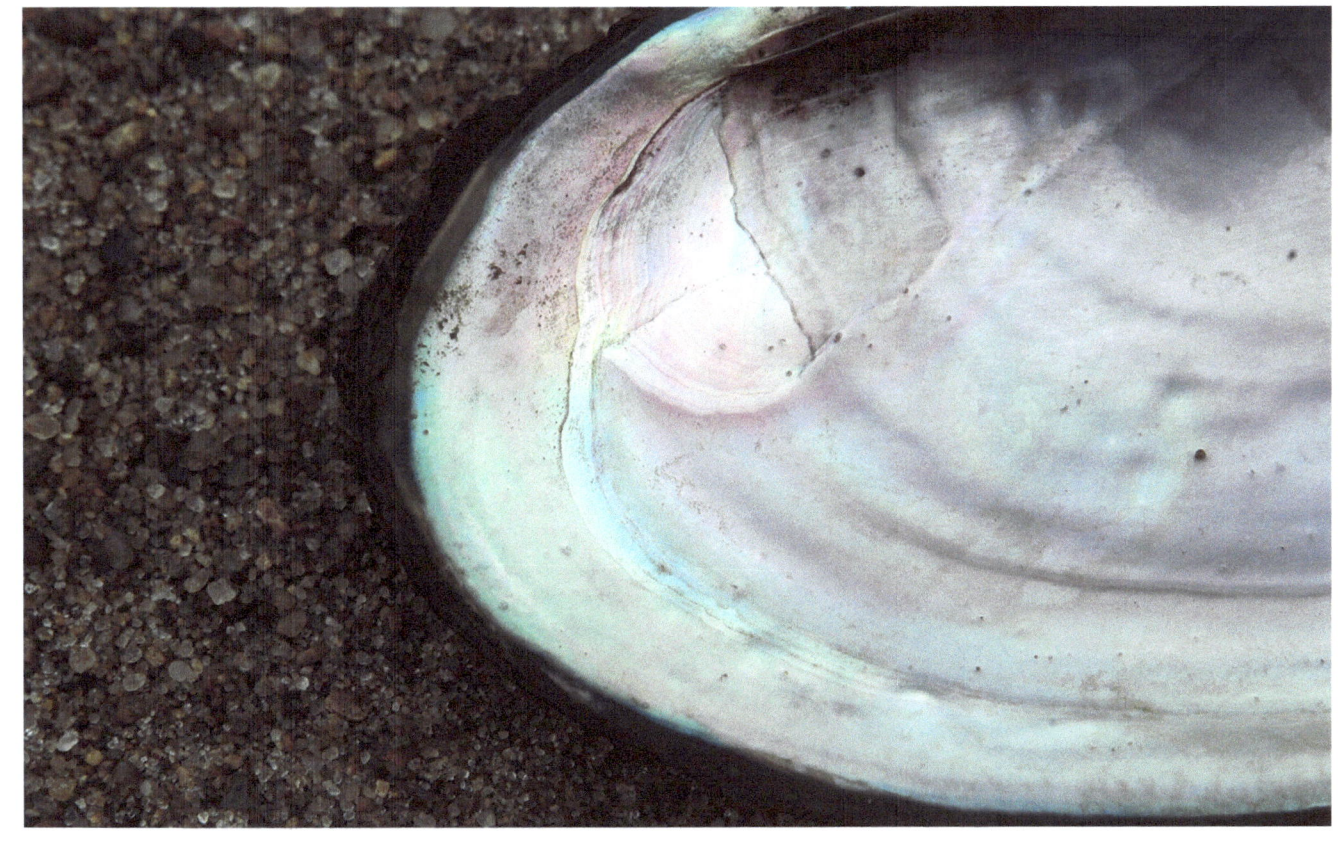

Shell of Fragile Papershell mussel
Segment 1, Jefferson County

86

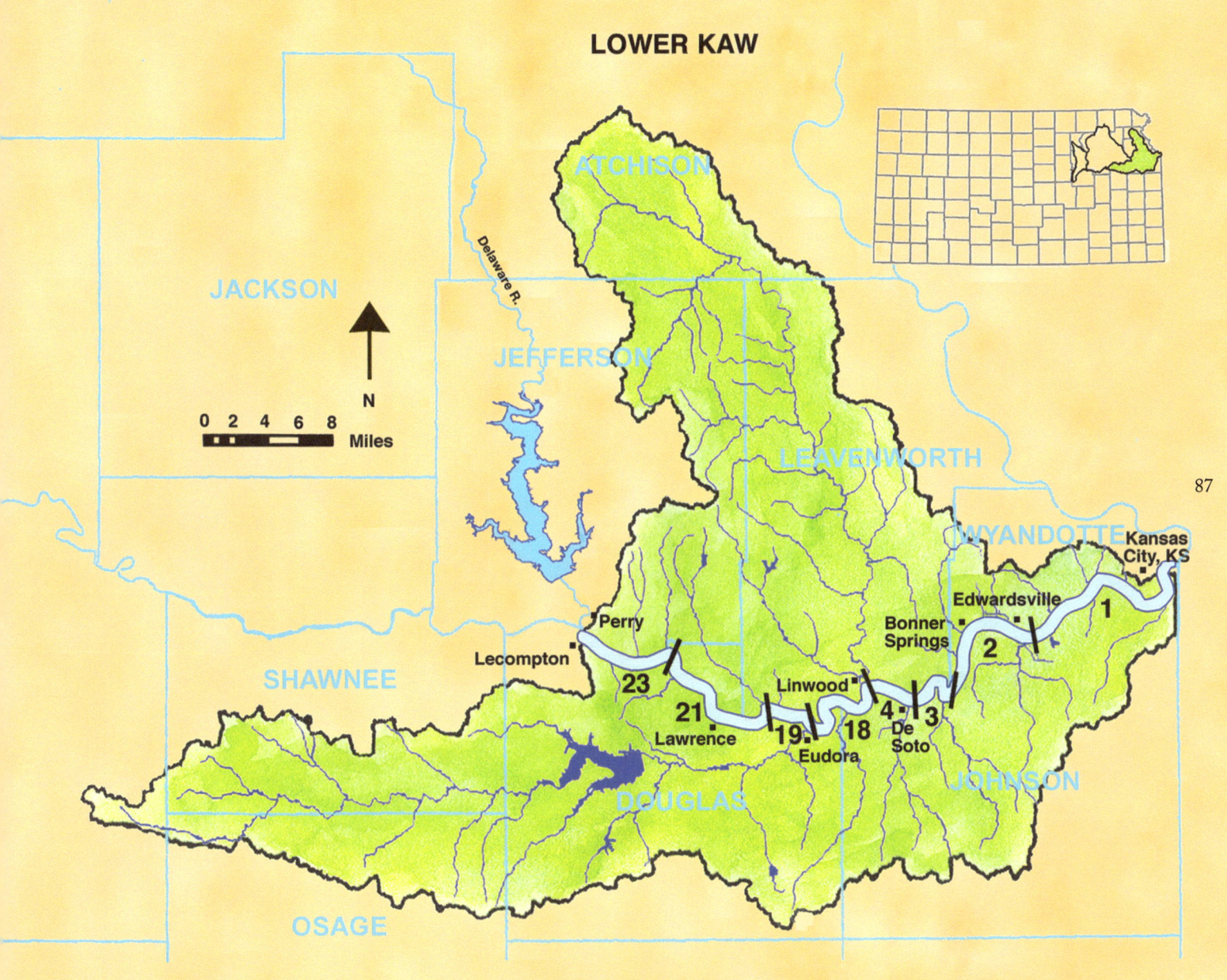

LOWER KAW

JACKSON

ATCHISON

Delaware R.

JEFFERSON

LEAVENWORTH

SHAWNEE

Perry

Lecompton

23

21

Lawrence

19

Eudora

Linwood

18

De Soto

4

3

Bonner Springs

Edwardsville

2

WYANDOTTE

Kansas City, KS

1

JOHNSON

DOUGLAS

OSAGE

0 2 4 6 8

N

Miles

87

THE KAW (KANSAS RIVER)
SEGMENTS 23, 21, 19, 18, 4, 3, 2, 1

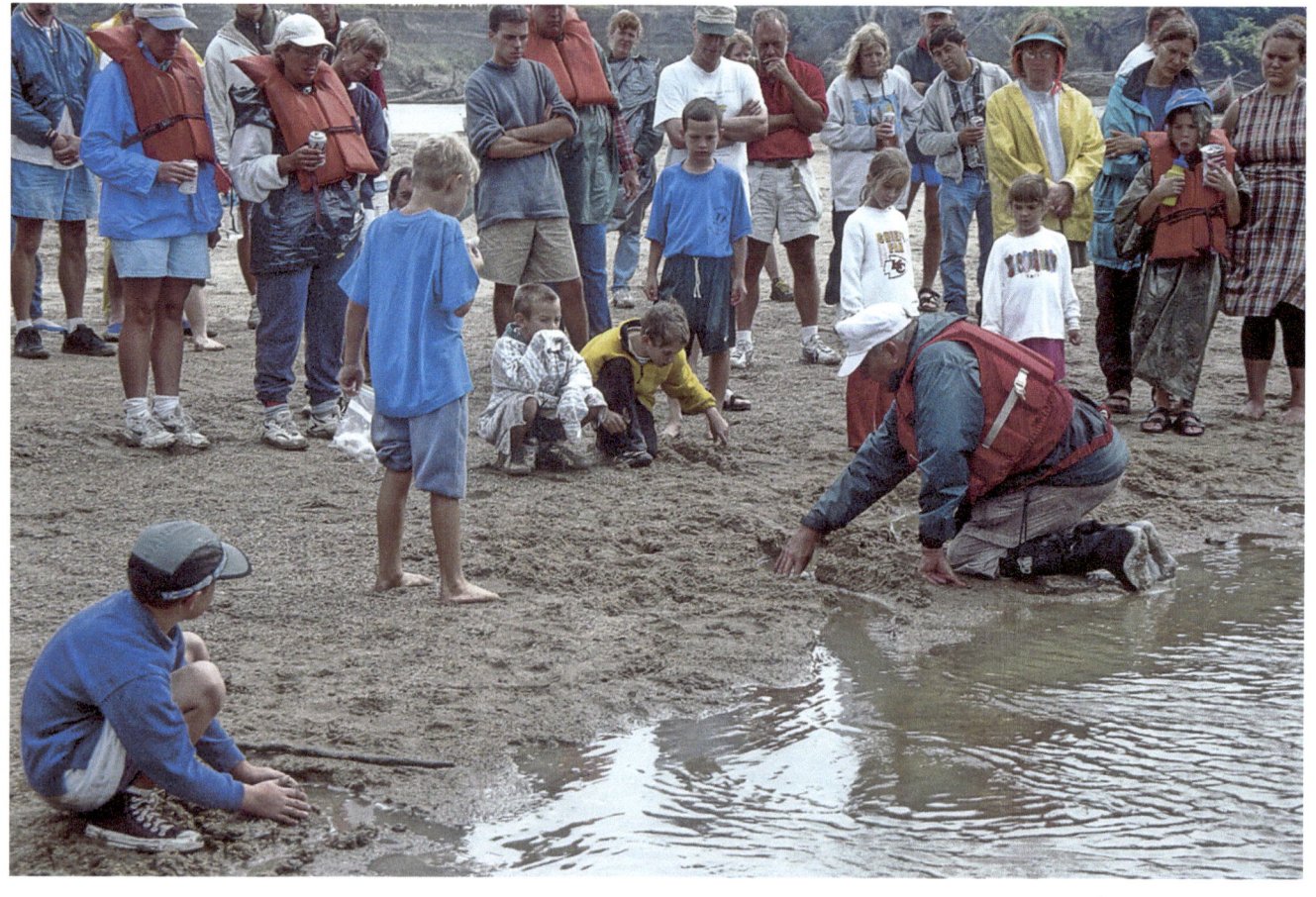

Kaw River 101
Segment 23, Douglas County

"FRIENDS OF THE KAW promotes the use of the river by hosting float trips and educating the public about safety and river conservation."

- Mike Calwell

"BACK IN THE LATE 70s I competed in the "KU - K-State" canoe race. The race was a blast, and the river was pristine with beautiful sand bars. Ah the Kaw - what great memories!"

- Jim Fleming

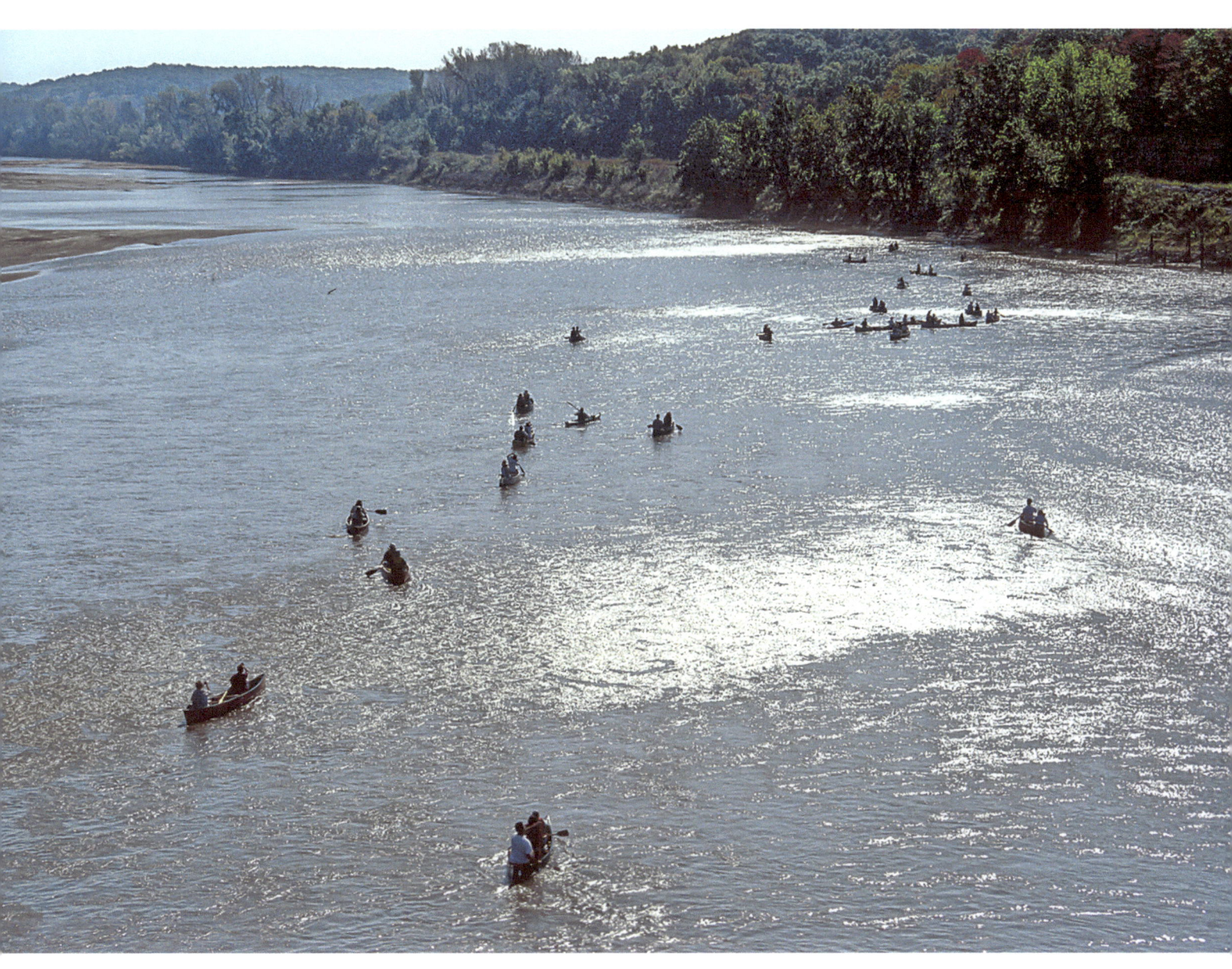

Float trip east of Lecompton
Segment 23, Douglas County

"SOME OF US are such dull folks that just stopping on a sand bar and poking around with a stick for old fossils can provide an hour's worth of excitement."

- Mike Ducey

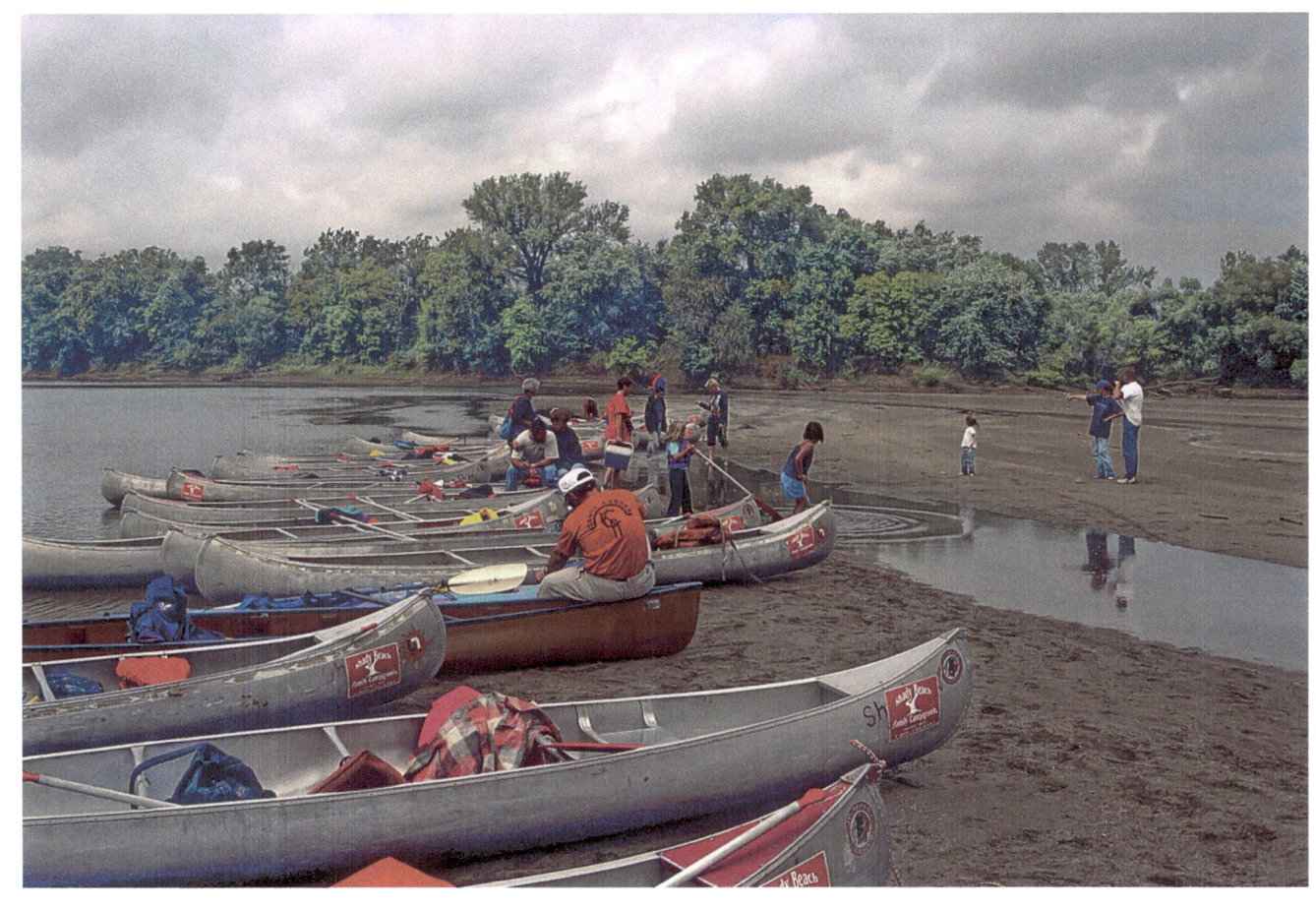

Sandbar rest stop
Segment 23, Jefferson County

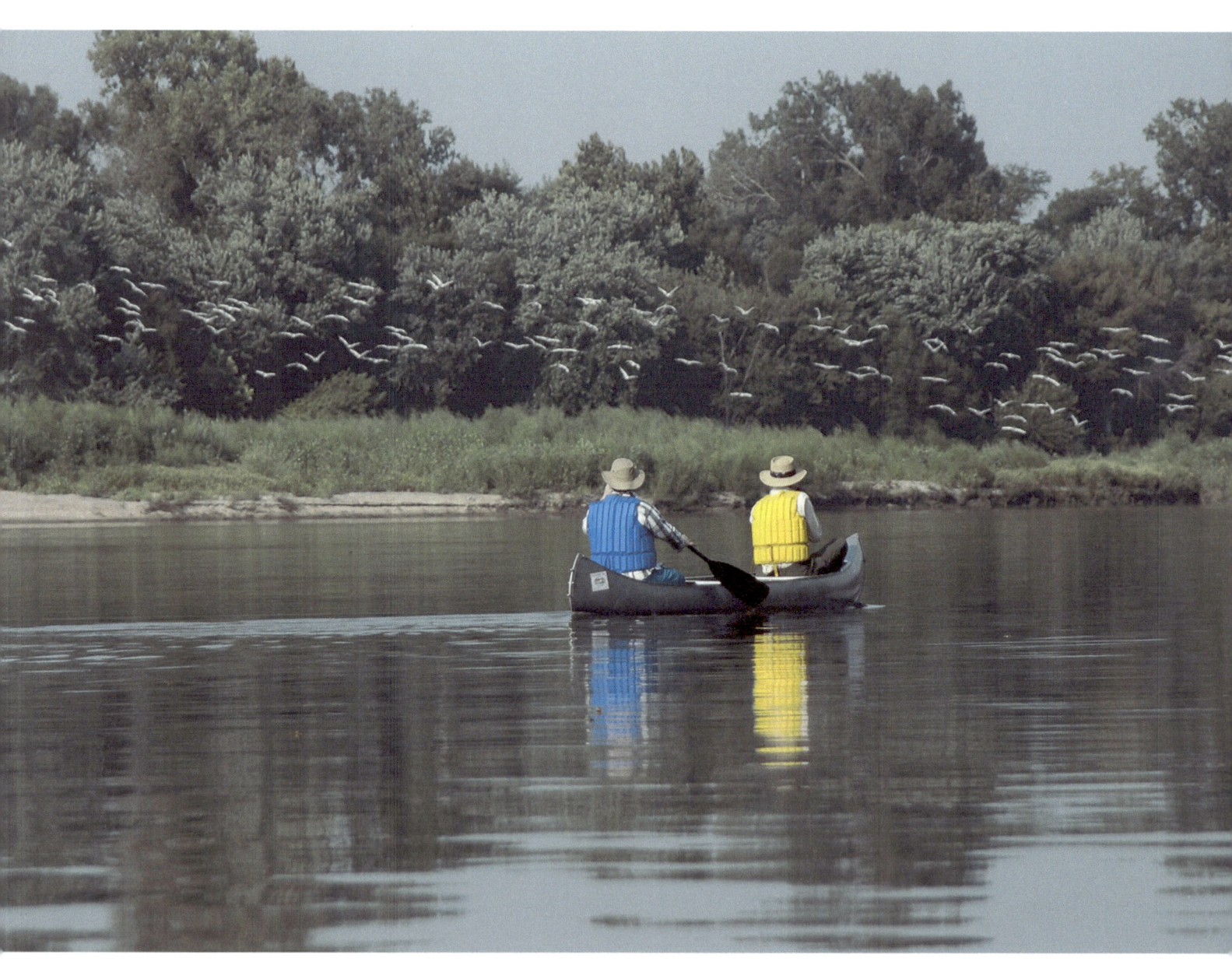

Two men and a canoe
Segment 23, Jefferson County

"THE KAW RIVER is a cherished refuge
from a connected, networked, full throttle world.
It is my opportunity to get off-line and on the river.
It is my time to connect with God, nature and sometimes
a few good friends, and often my setting for personal
reflection and examination."

- R. J. Stephenson

"ONE OF MY FAVORITE pastimes is back country camping on a Kaw River sandbar."

- Laura Calwell

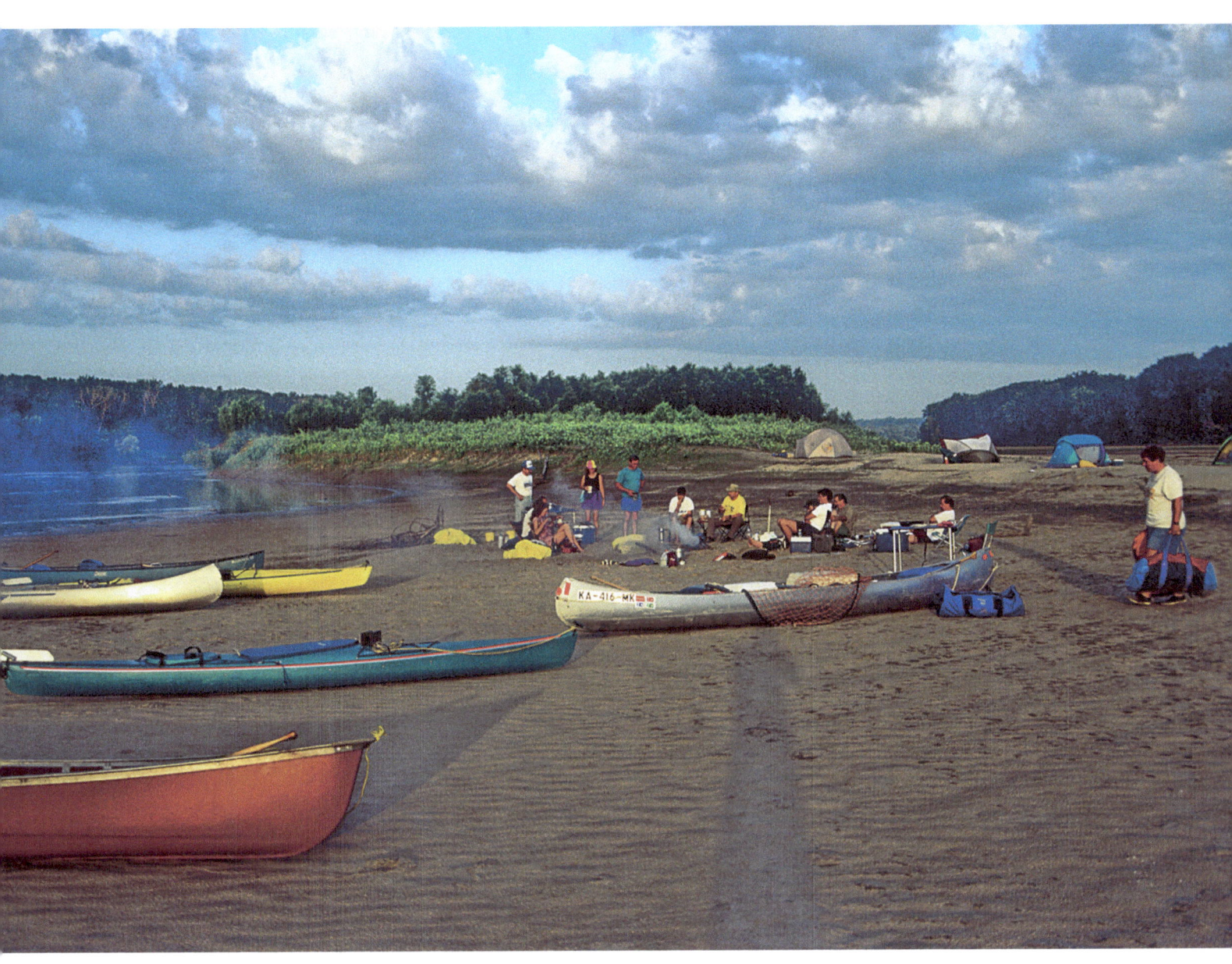

Early morning campsite
Segment 23, Jefferson County

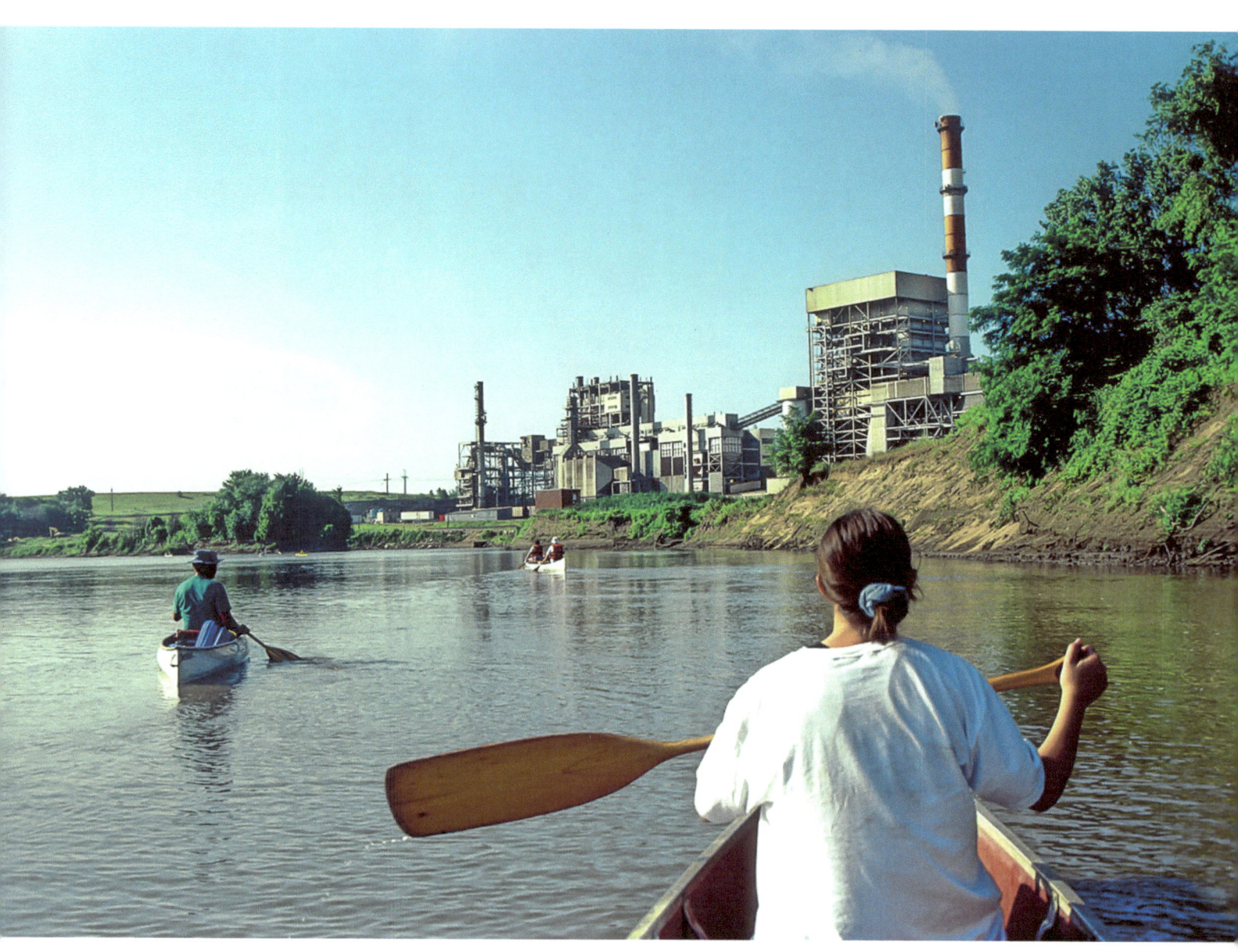

Passing by the Lawrence Energy Center
Segment 21, Douglas County

"IF YOU WANT TO KNOW eastern Kansas, know the Kaw. It cuts through fertile farm fields, passes by small and large communities, yields sand for infrastructure, powers generators for electricity, provides water for multiple uses, accepts the runoff from cities and farms, and serves as a backdoor for all to see the positive and negative effects of our society."

- Hank Ernst

(overleaf)
Summer sunset on the Kaw
Segment 21, Douglas County

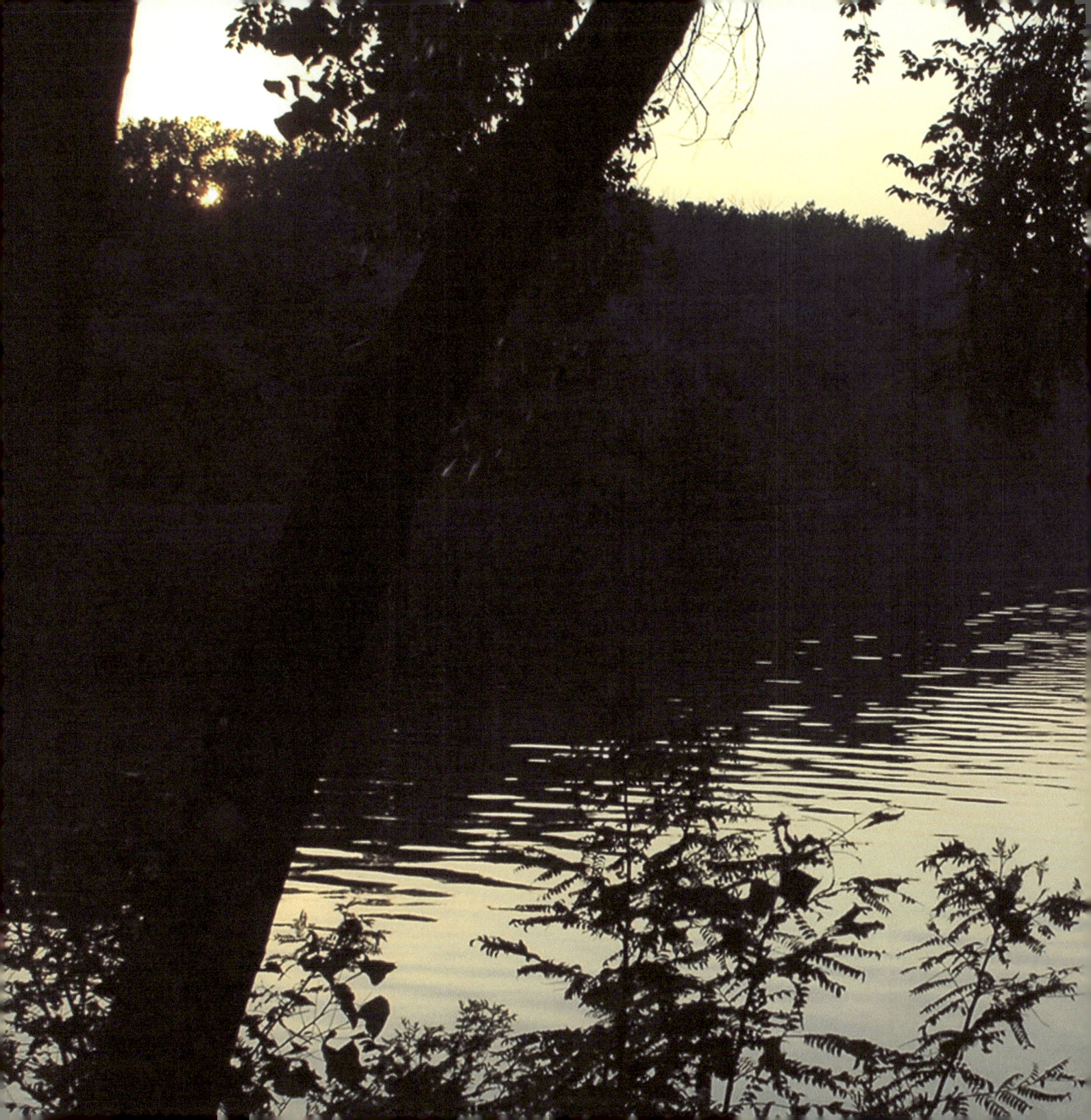

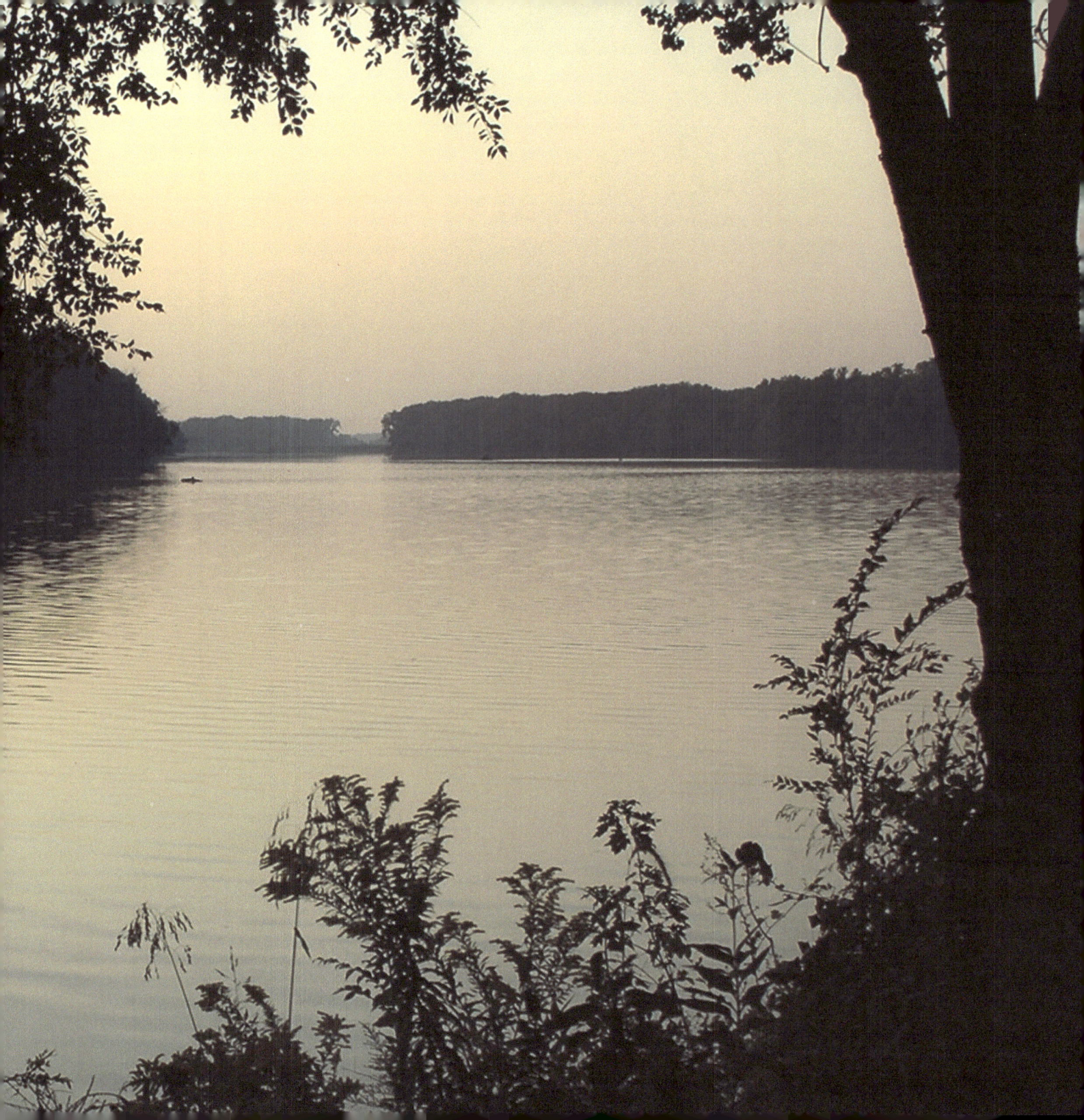

Saturday crew races at Burcham Park
Segment 21, Douglas County

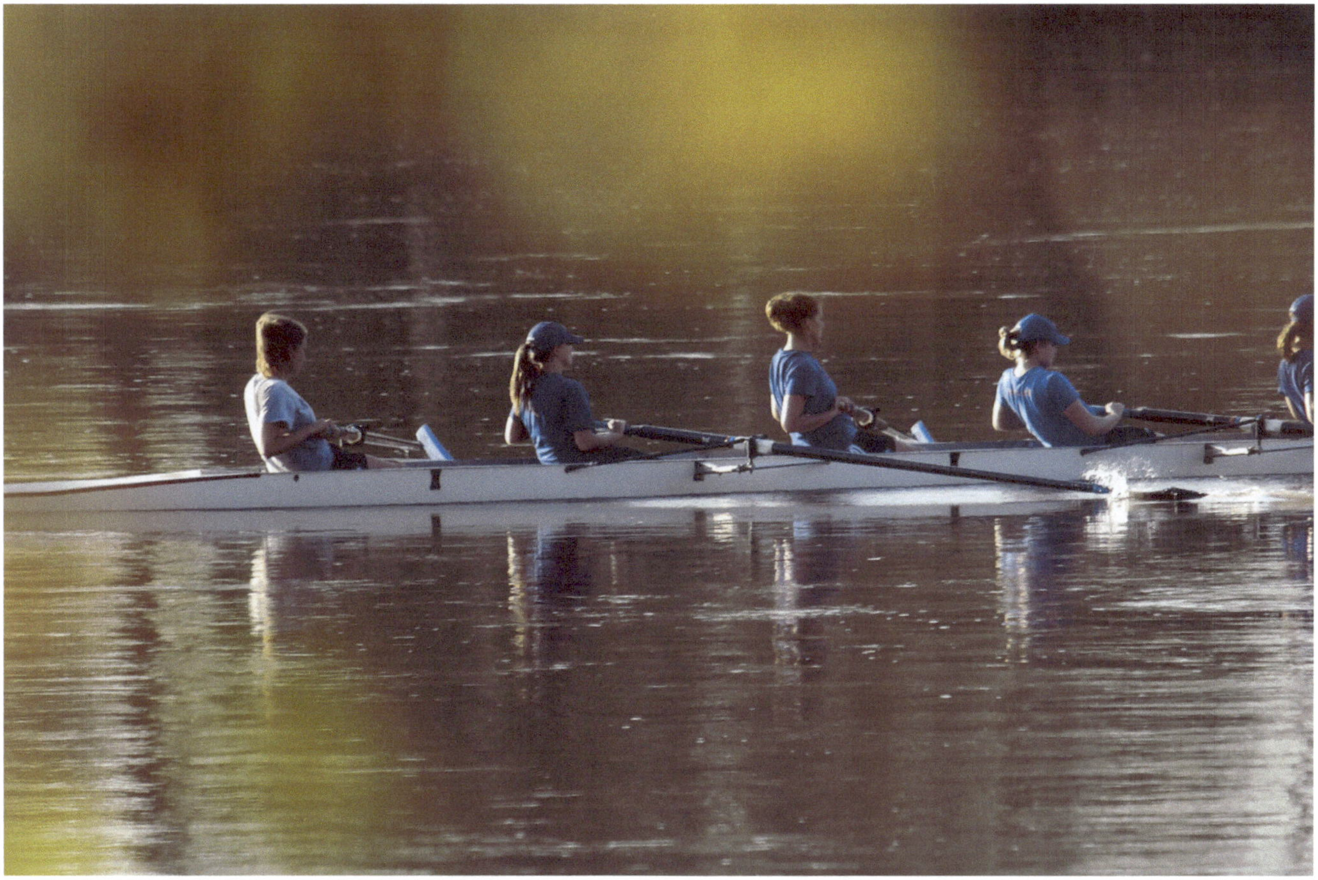

Crew girls on the Kaw
Segment 21, Douglas County

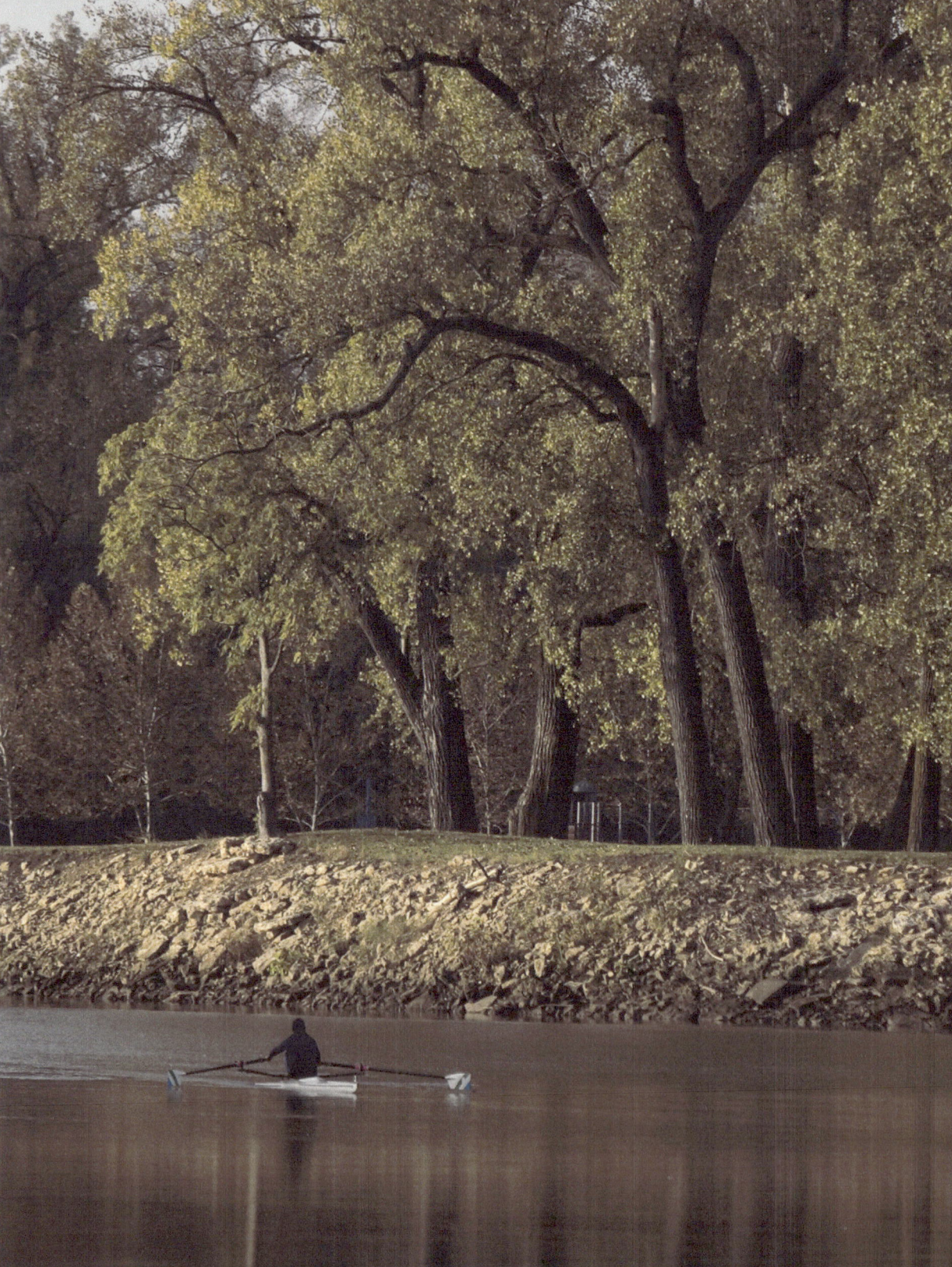

"SOMETIMES ON A RIVER crowded with college rowers, most often alone, from early March to late November, I scull the 3 mile stretch of the Kaw upstream from the Bowersock Dam. Endless strokes, countless laps, but never boredom. Each stroke makes demands of strength, grace, and mindfulness. The straining legs, back, arms and meditative rhythm connects me to my Kaw; there is adventure in repetition. A pause to drink or rest between hard pieces offers moments to admire the Egrets, or in summer the shore birds on sand bars, or in fall the return of the Eagles telling me my days on the river are soon to end, until next March.**"

- Steven Maynard-Moody

Rowing near Burcham Park
Segment 21, Douglas County

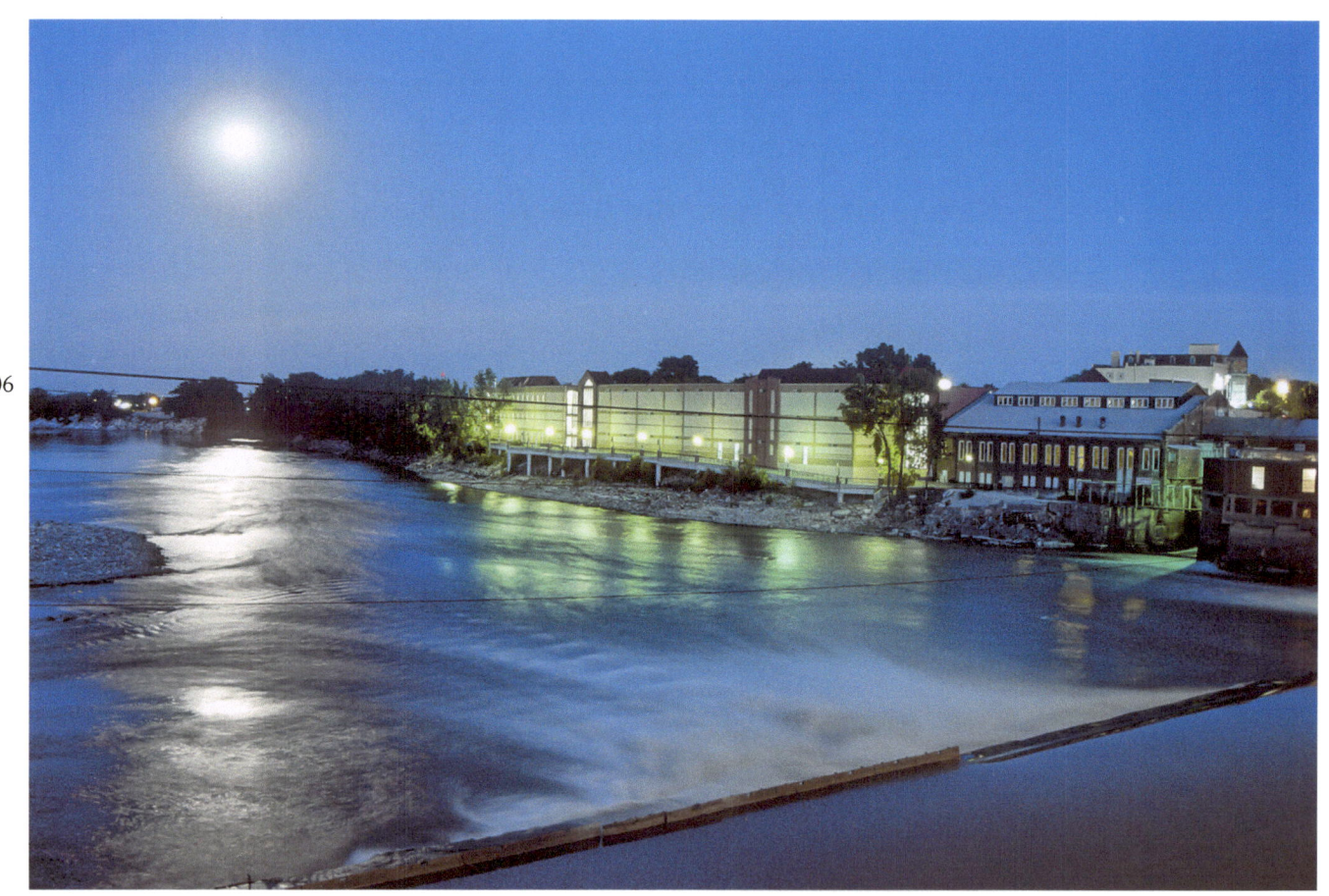

Lawrence riverfront at moonrise
Segment 21, Douglas County

"THE SOFT LIGHT of a full moon glistens on the Kaw River."

- Erlene Slingsby

"AS A BOY, I rode my bicycle along it, camped beside it and fished in it long before anyone worried about pollution. My friends and I caught catfish, spoonbills, sturgeon, and many other varieties of fish."

- William (Tom) Stull

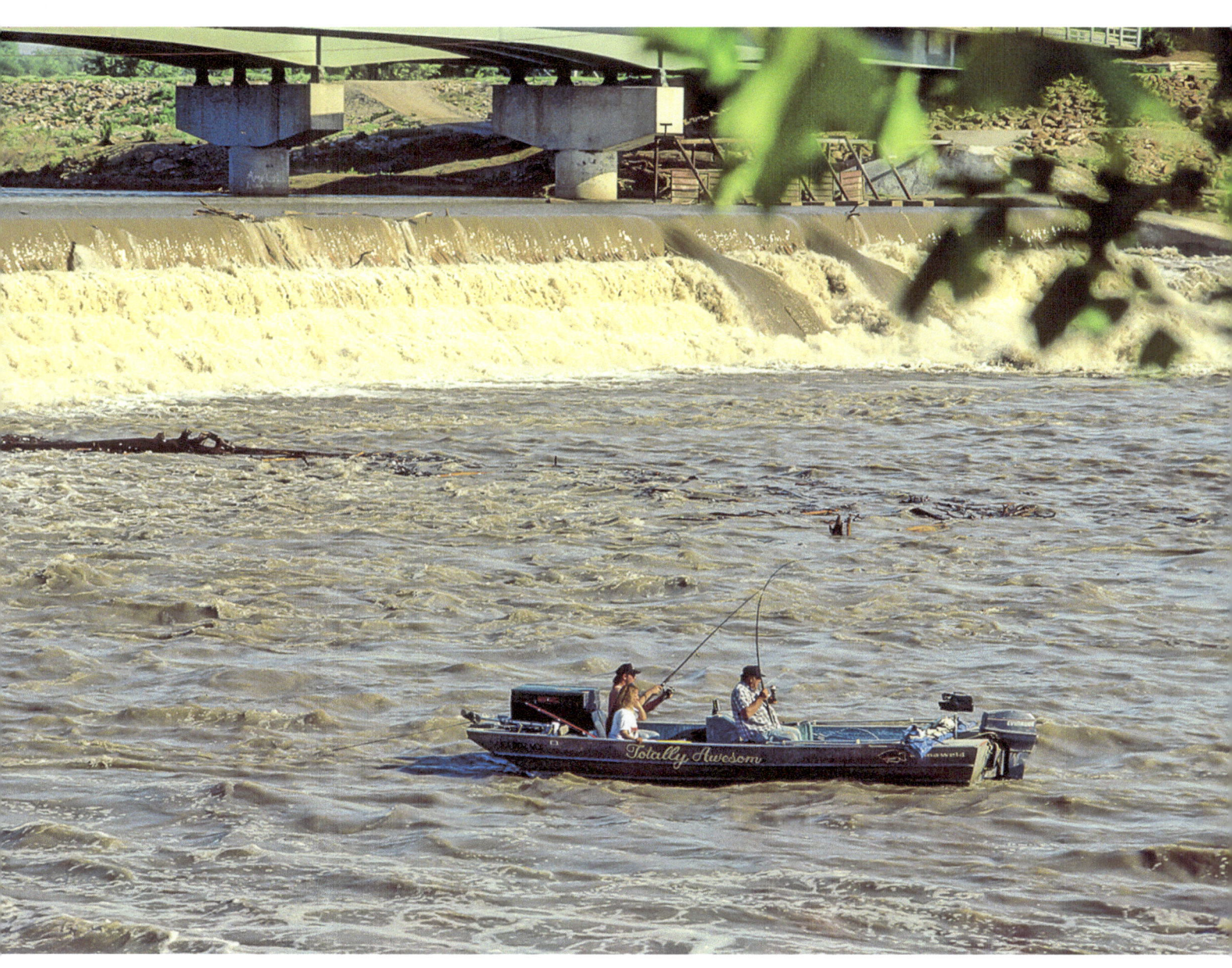

Fishing below Bowersock Dam
Segment 21, Douglas County

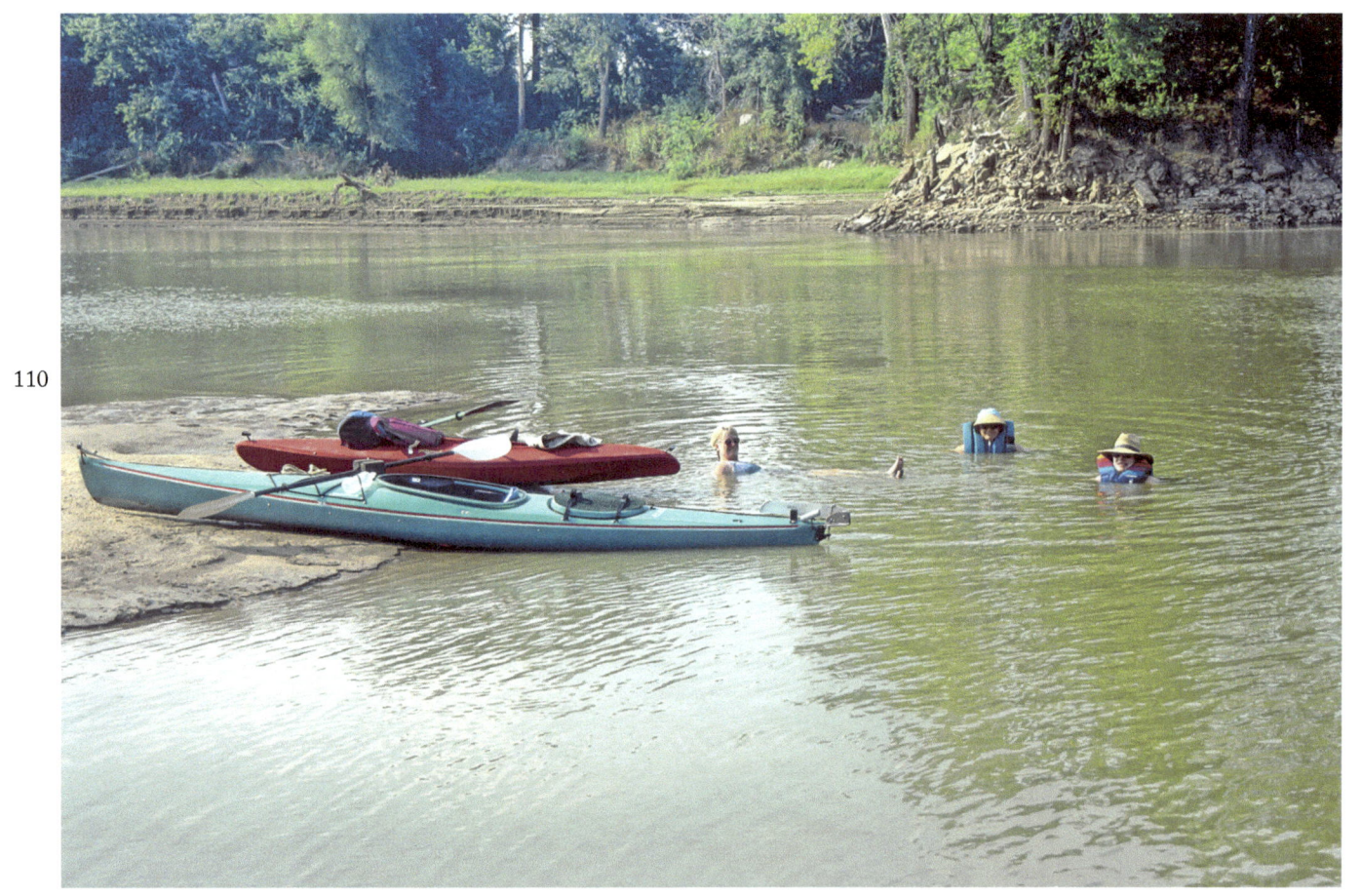

Enjoying a soak
Segment 19, Douglas County

"AFTER A DAY of paddling, going for a soak in the river is the best."

- Chip Farley

(overleaf)
Quiet stretch of the Kaw
Segment 19, Leavenworth County

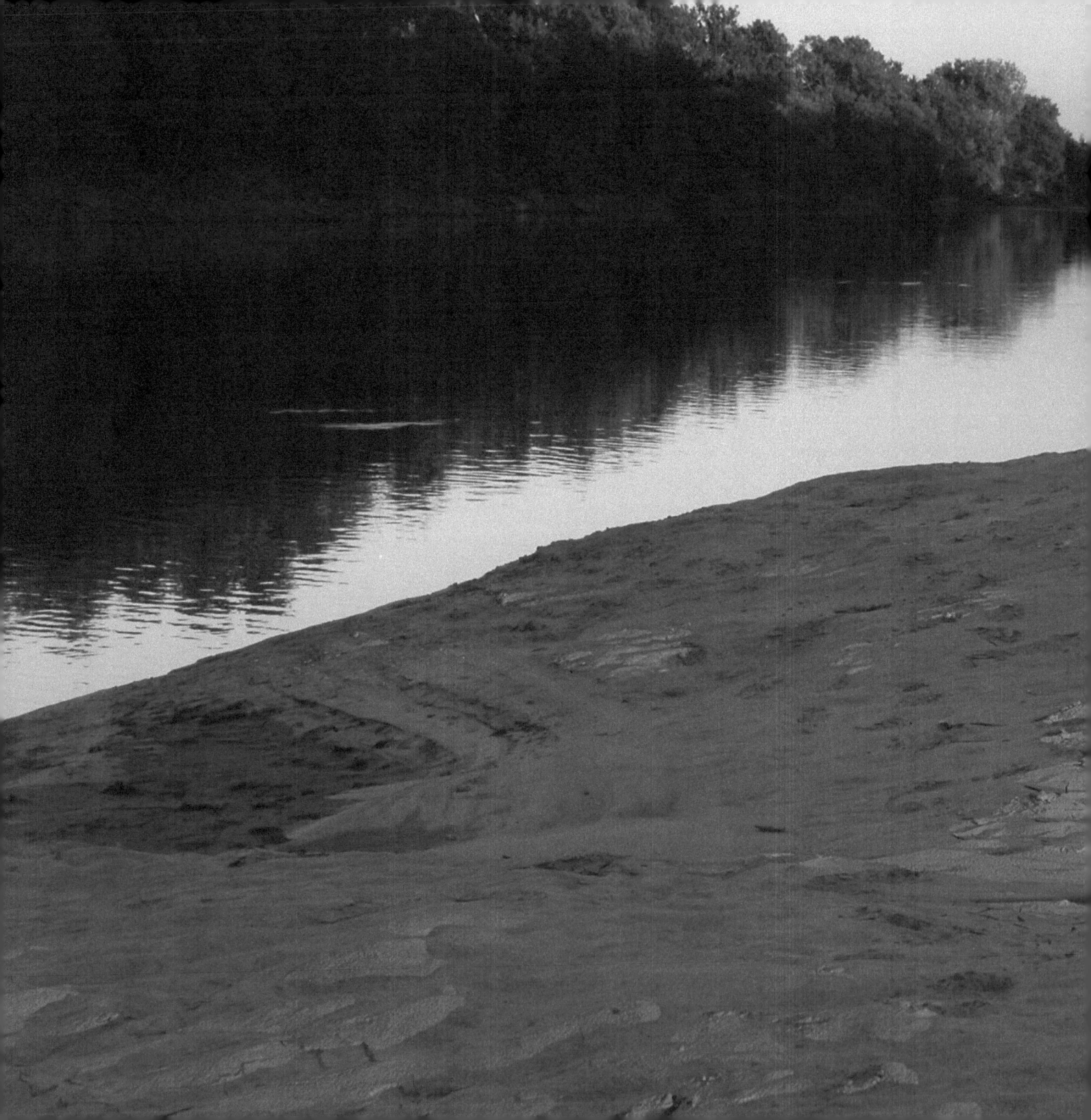

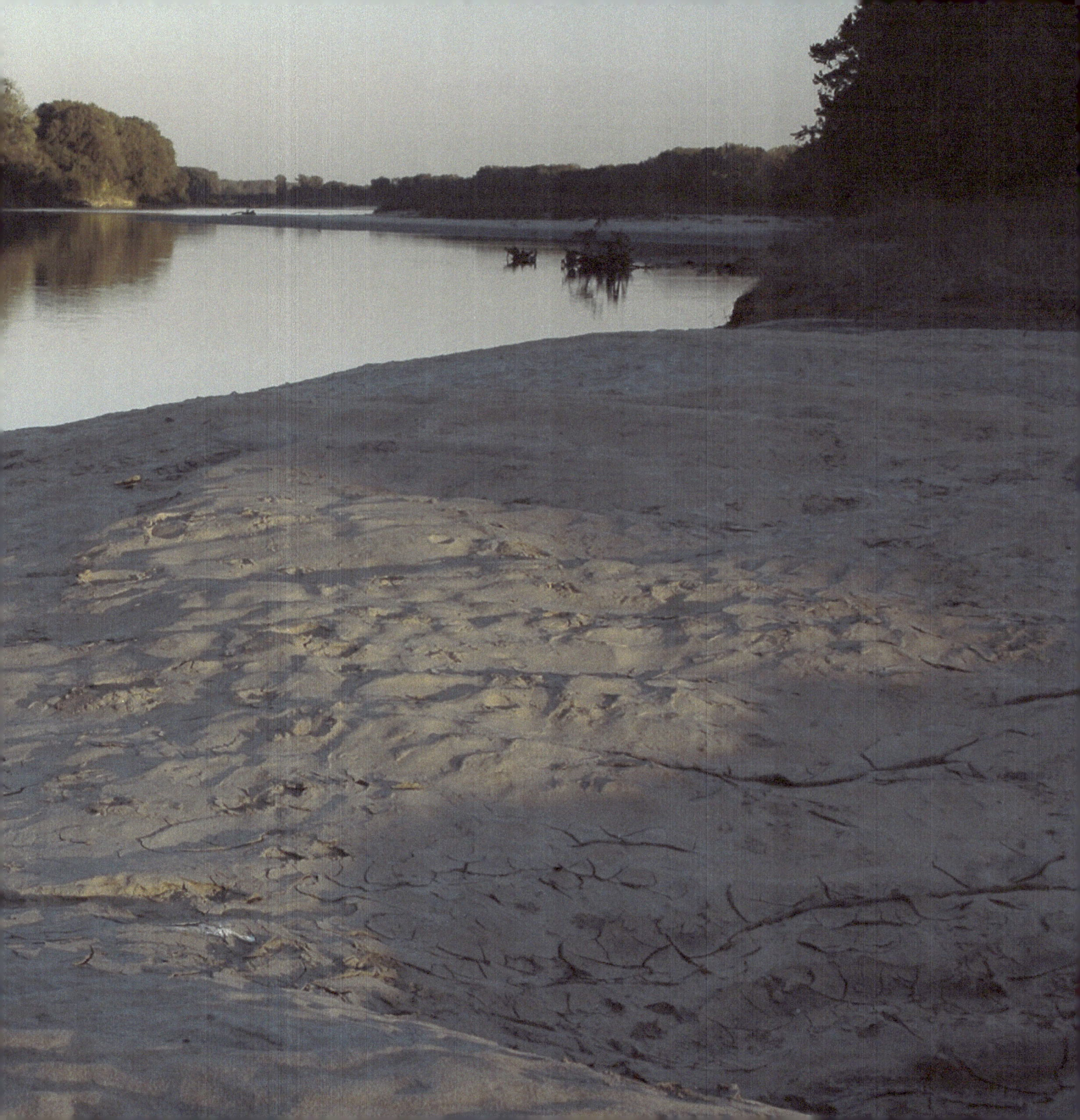

"EVERYONE HAS FAVORITE PLACES they can't do without. I need the Kaw River. I need to float its channel quietly, be around its wildlife; I need to camp overnight on its sandbars and watch sunsets, the moon and stars above, sunrises, weather changes, all of these on a regular basis, and year-round, else life just doesn't feel right.**"**

- Joe Hyde

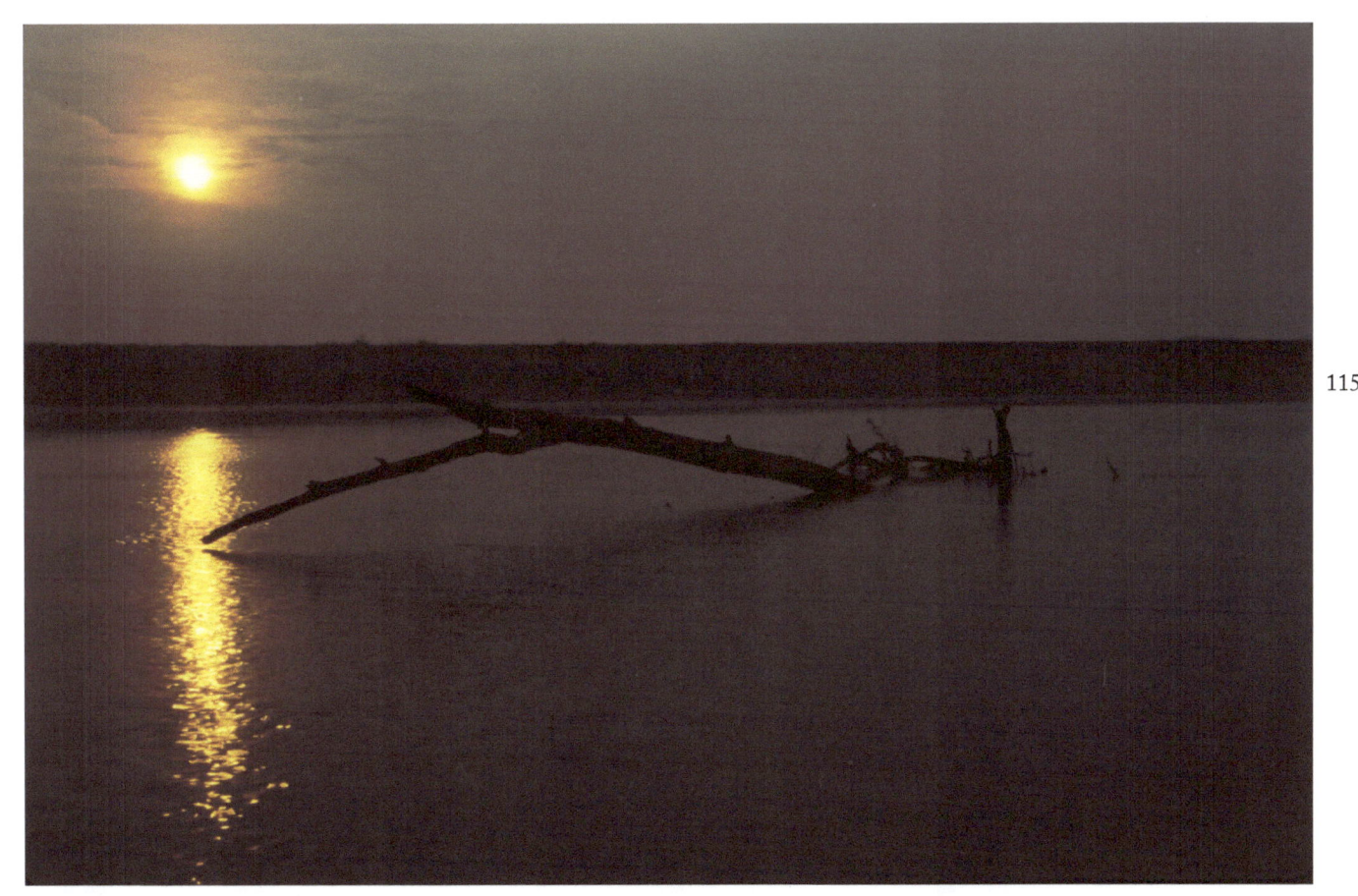

Cottonwood branch at sunrise
Segment 18, Douglas County

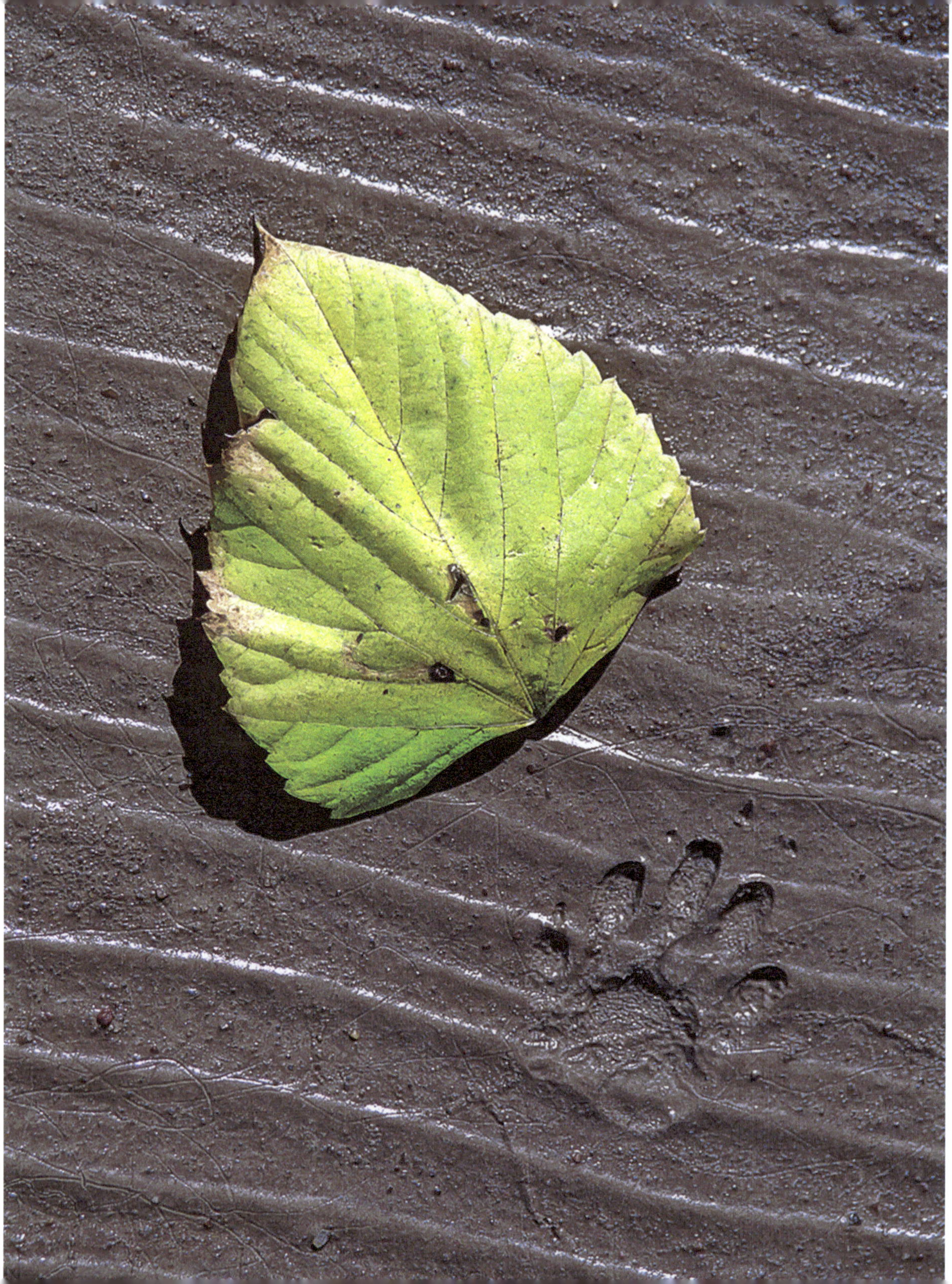

"I CAN REMEMBER going to the river with my friends back when bikes and parents were our only modes of transportation. We'd aimlessly wander the sandbars in search of anything that might satisfy the curiosity of an inquisitive young boy. It was nothing like the toys and games that inevitably lost our attention. The river's majesty has persisted through the years and I still find myself longing for its presence.**"**

- Derek Fuller

117

(opposite)
Raccoon paw print and leaf
Segment 18, Johnson County

(overleaf)
Following the leader
Segment 4, Leavenworth County

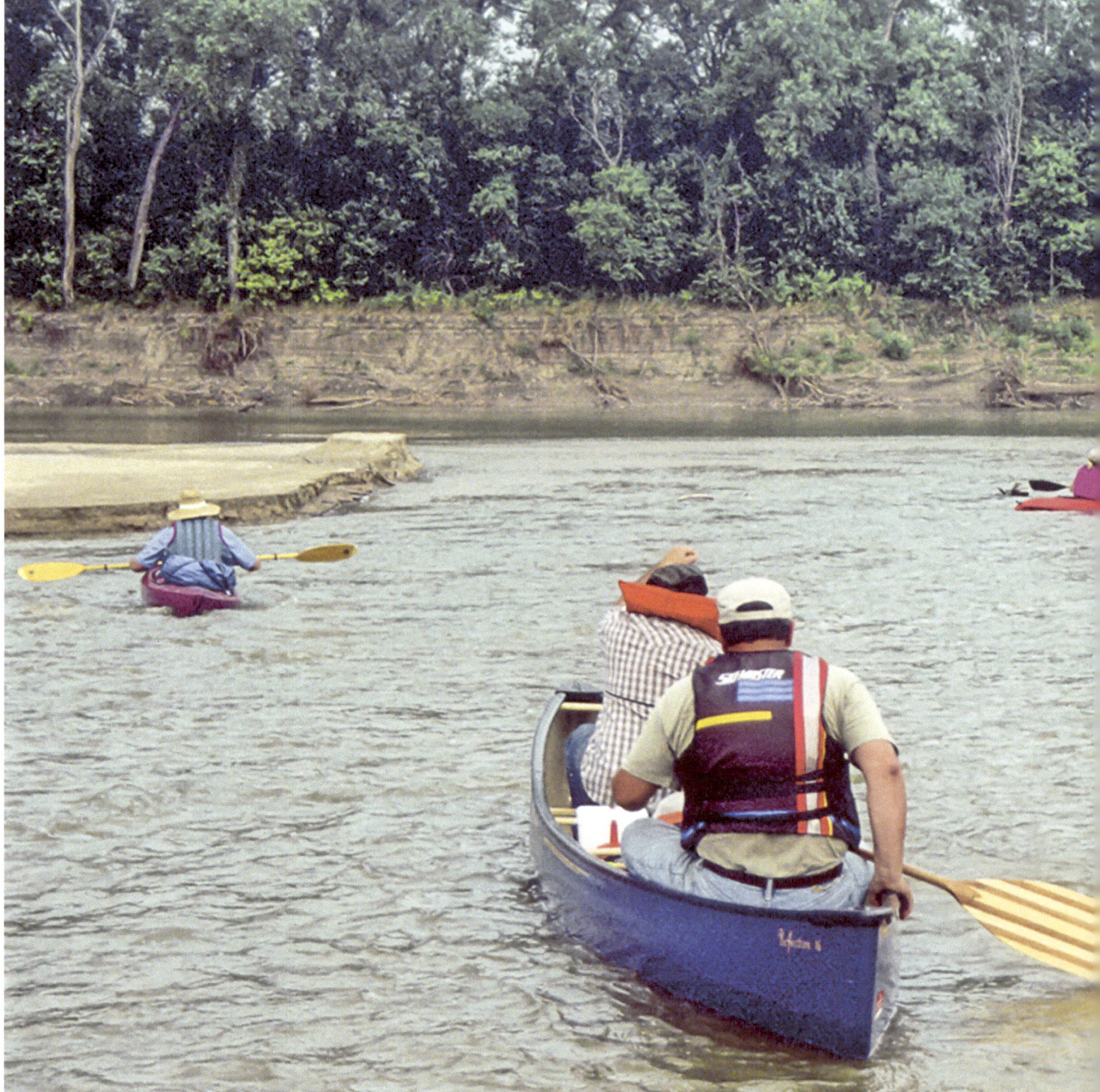

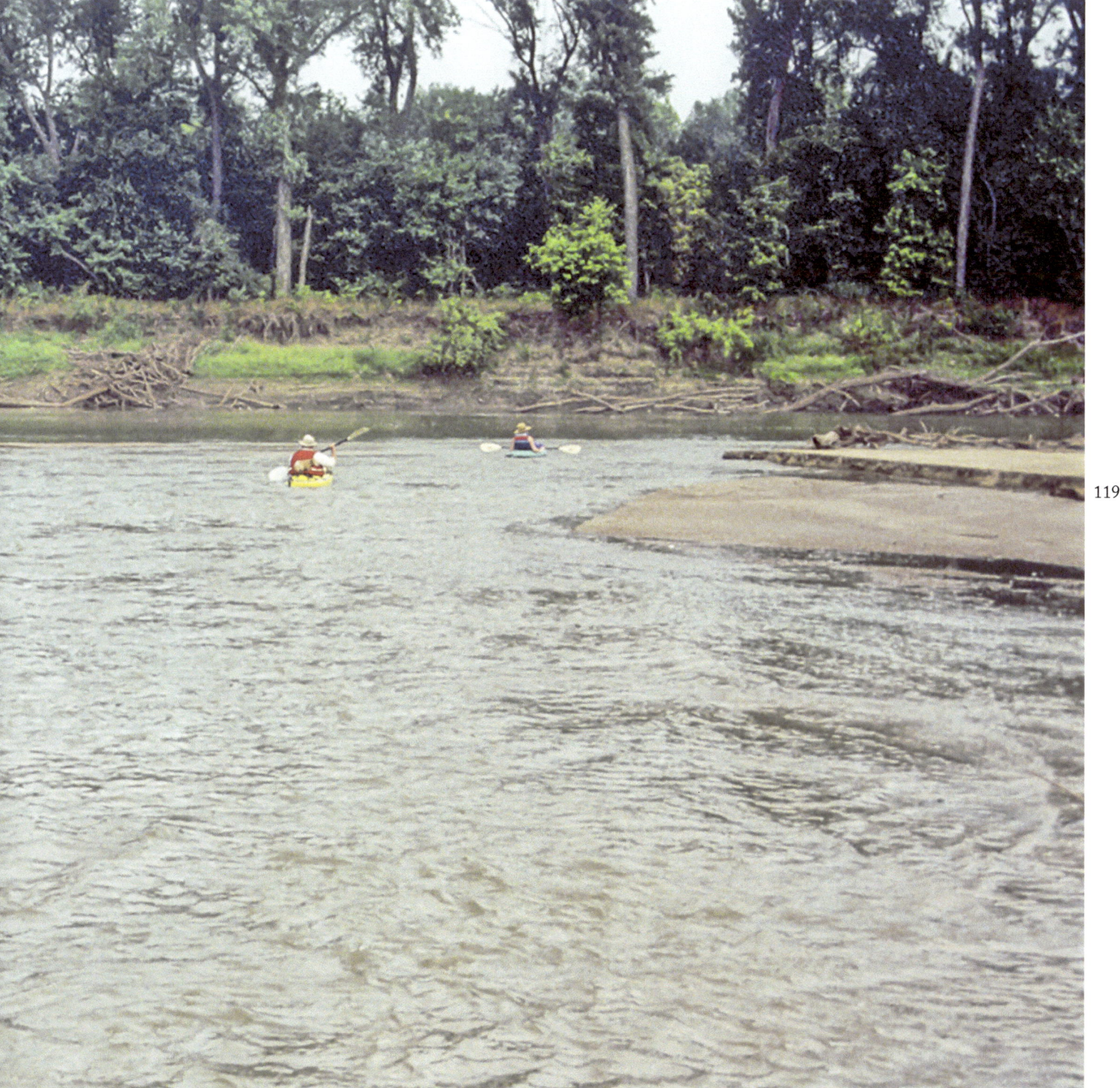

Racers in the "Gritty Fitty" from Lawrence to KC
Segment 4, Johnson County

Sandbank on bend
Segment 3, Johnson County

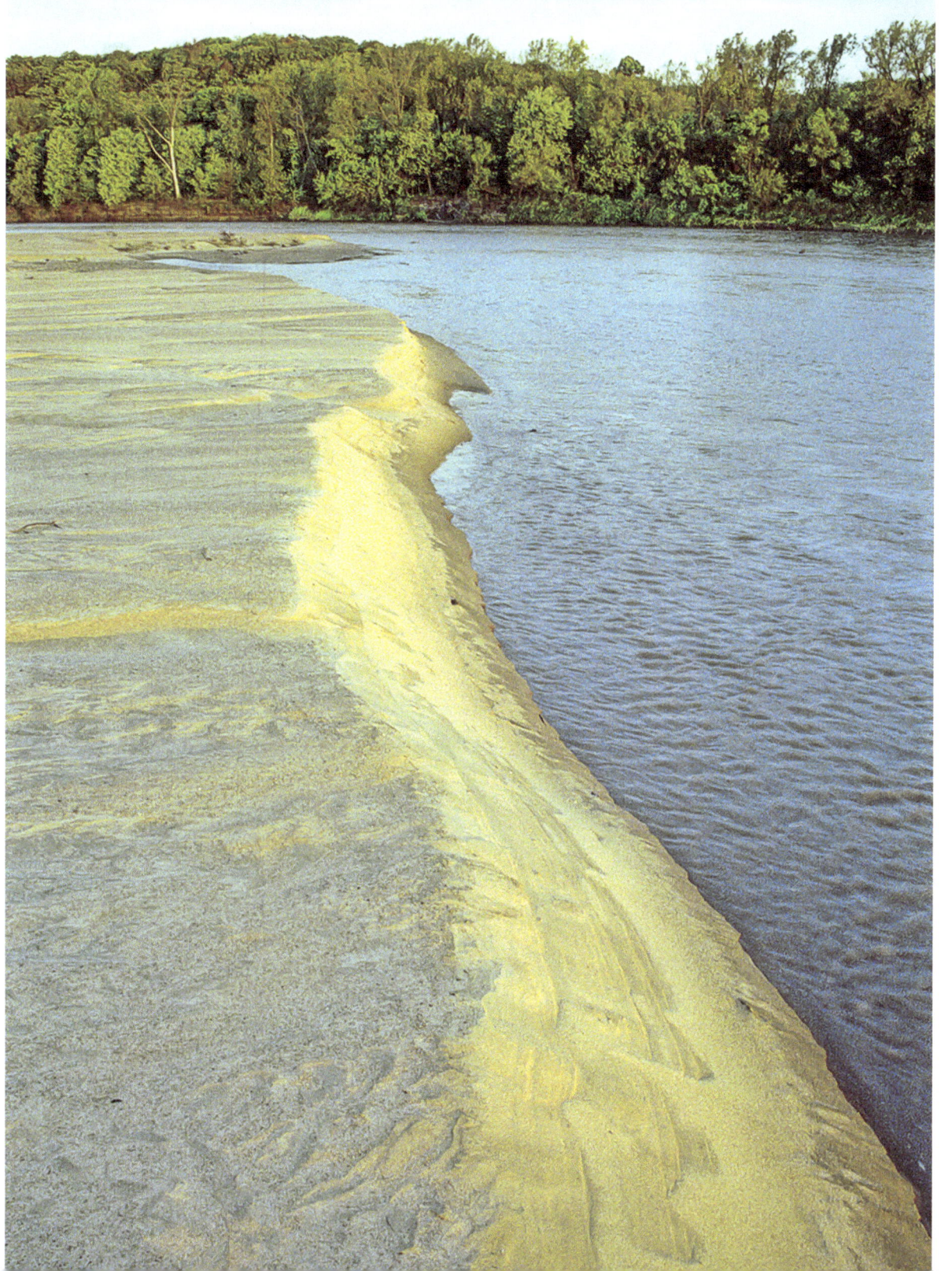

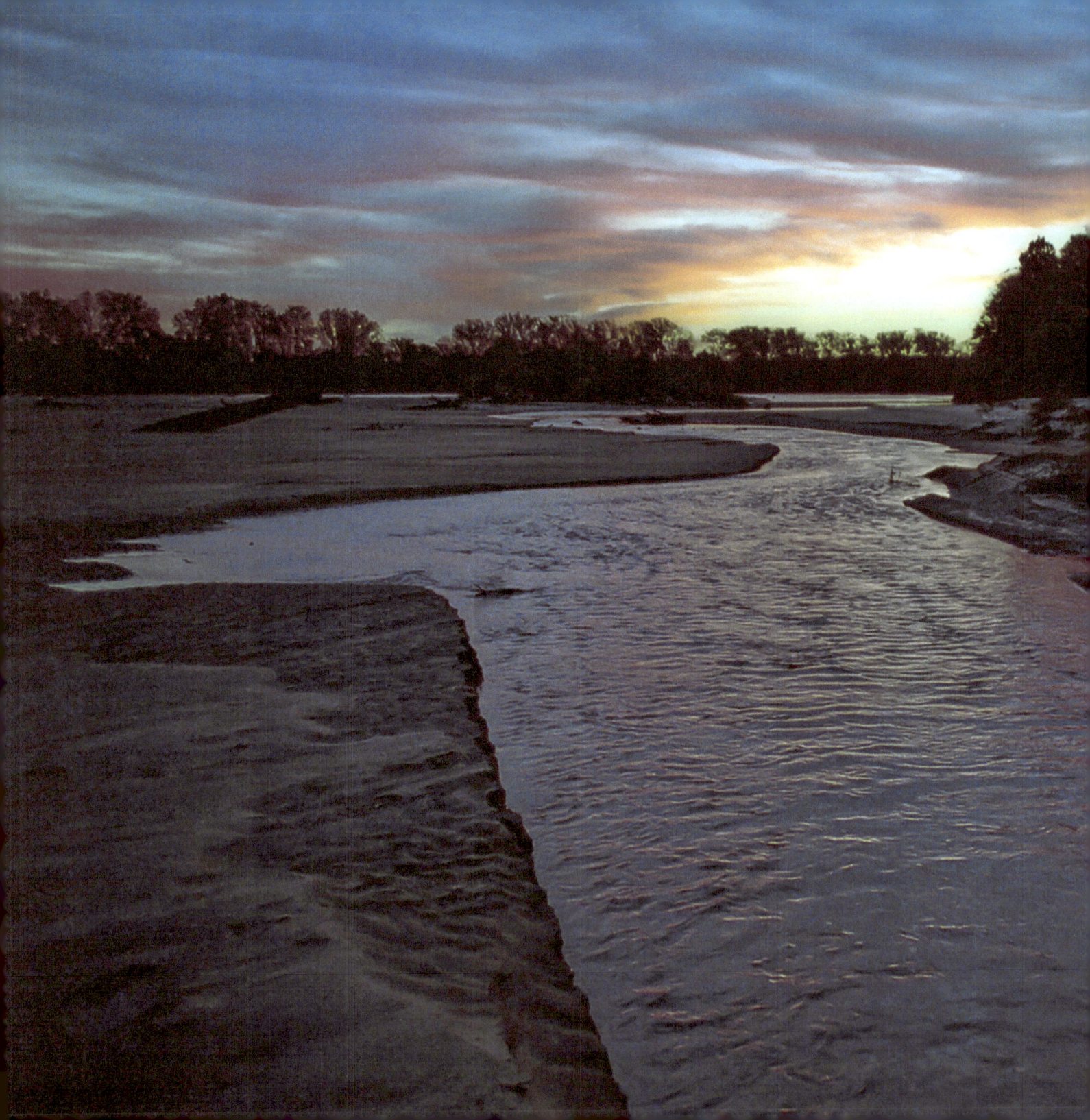

"I LOVE RIVER WORDS:
bends and bars, shoals, snags,
and floodplain scrolls, reaches
and roils, eddies, currents
and braided channels, not
to mention towheads,
cutoffs, and oxbows.**"**

- Lisa Grossman

123

The meandering Kaw
Segment 3, Johnson County

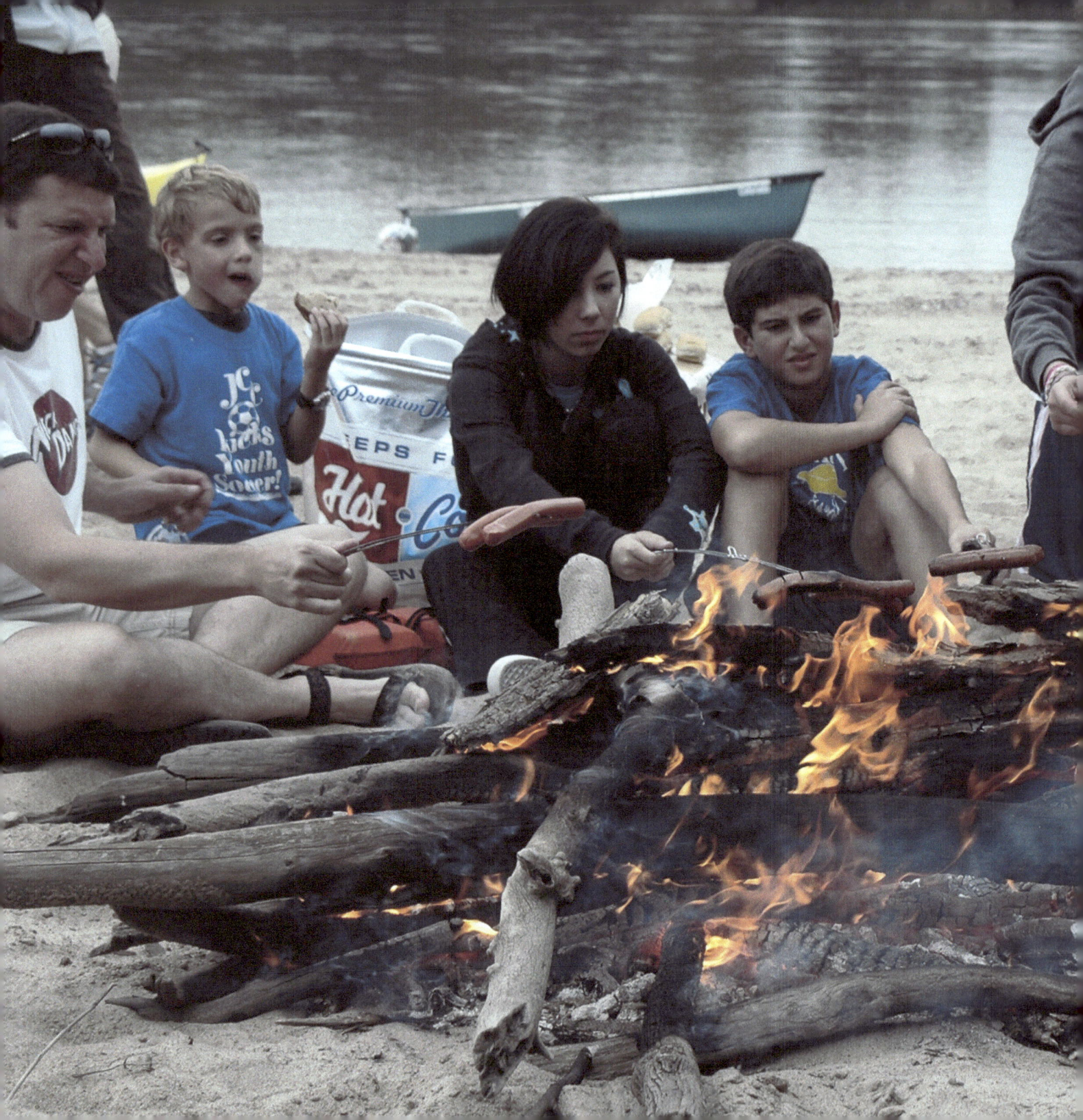

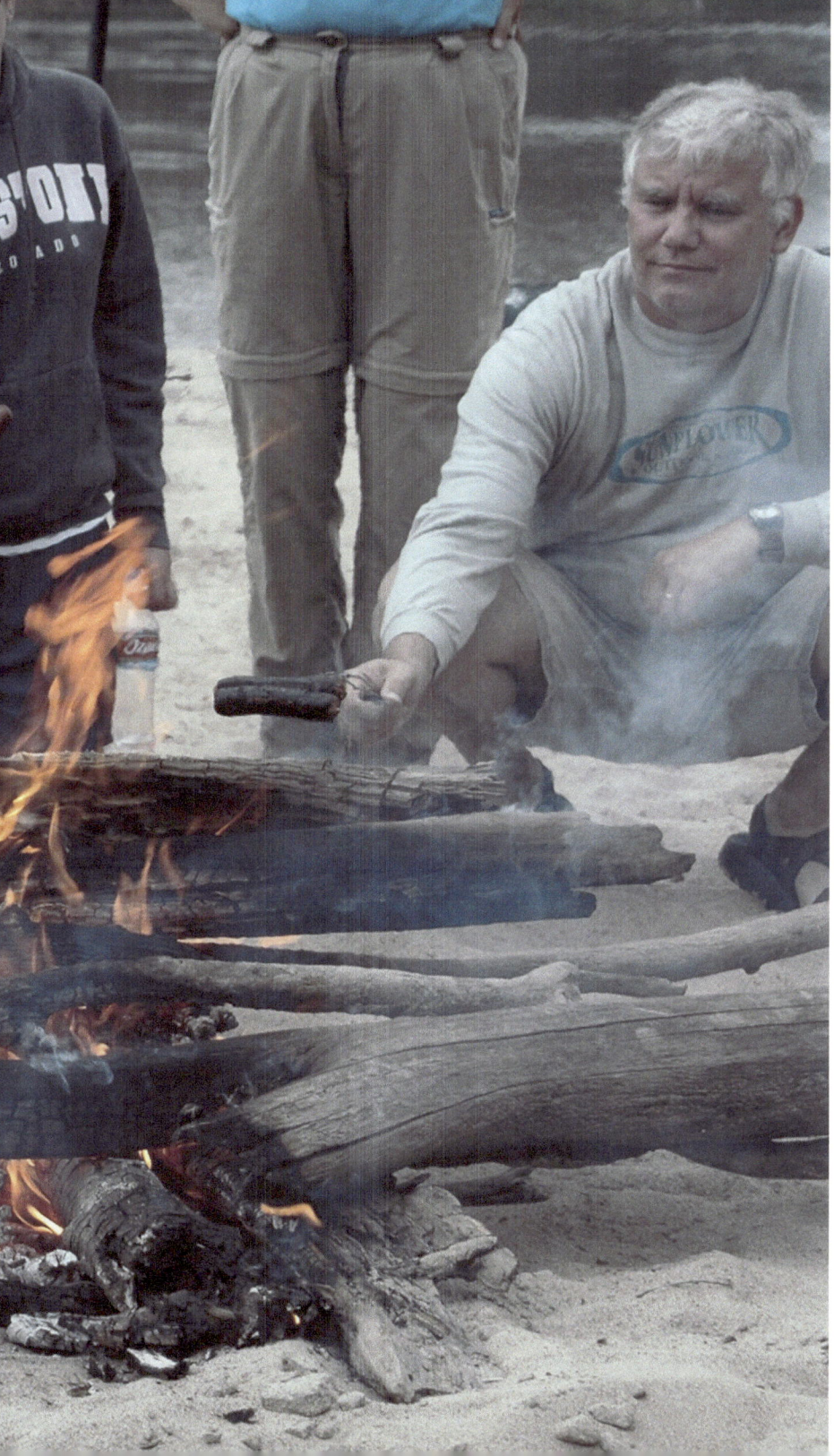

❝I HAVE FOUND that sharing my outdoor experiences with a youngster is a great excuse to leave the office and chores behind and to relax and rediscover some of the simple joys of outdoor fun.❞

- Stephen Garlow

Hot dog roasting
Segment 3, Leavenworth County

"THE KISS OF MY PADDLE dipping into the water combined with that occasional splash against the bow of my kayak are the subtle reasons that draw me to experience the rewarding time spent on this river, my old love and friend for life."

- Gregory Newlin

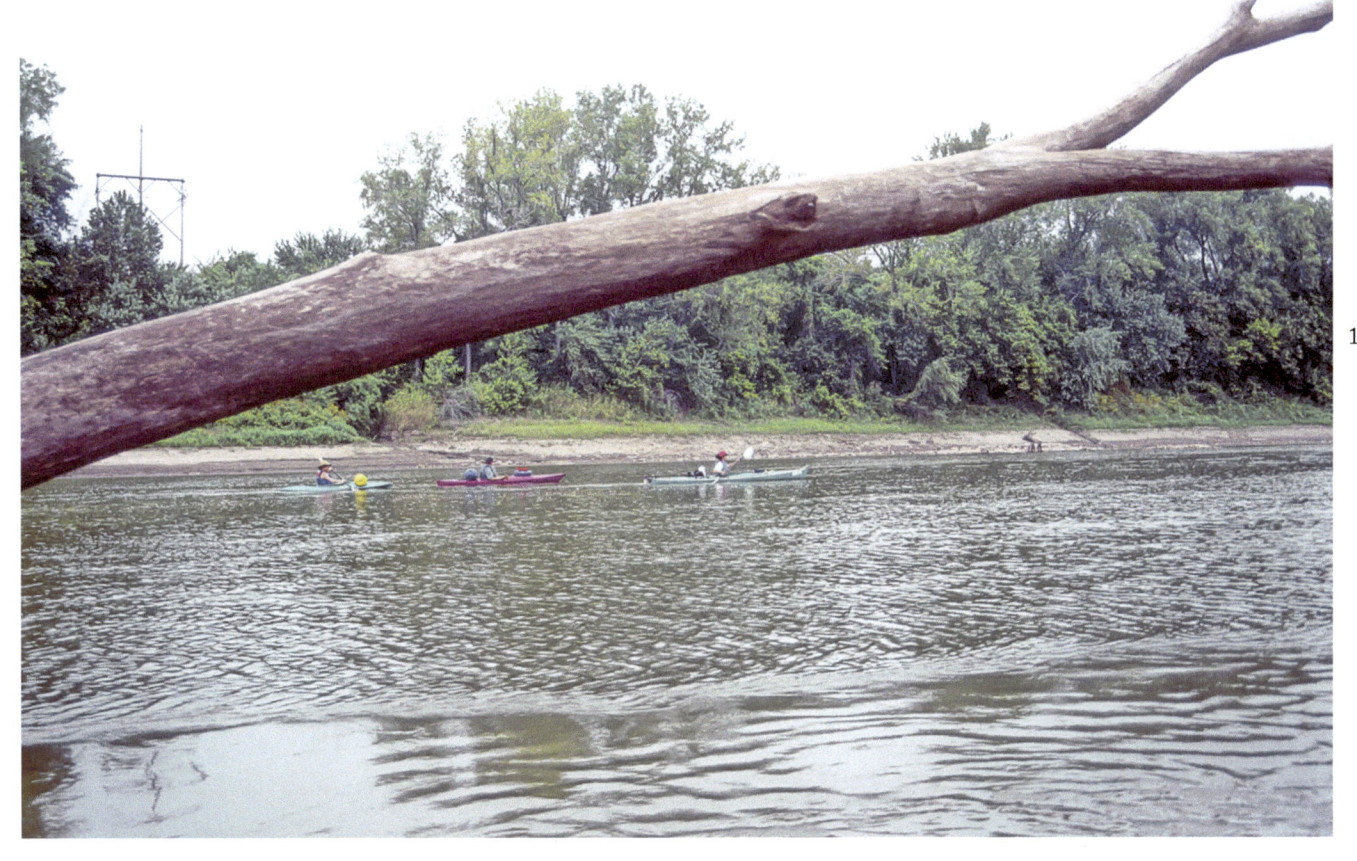

Three kayakers
Segment 2, Wyandotte County

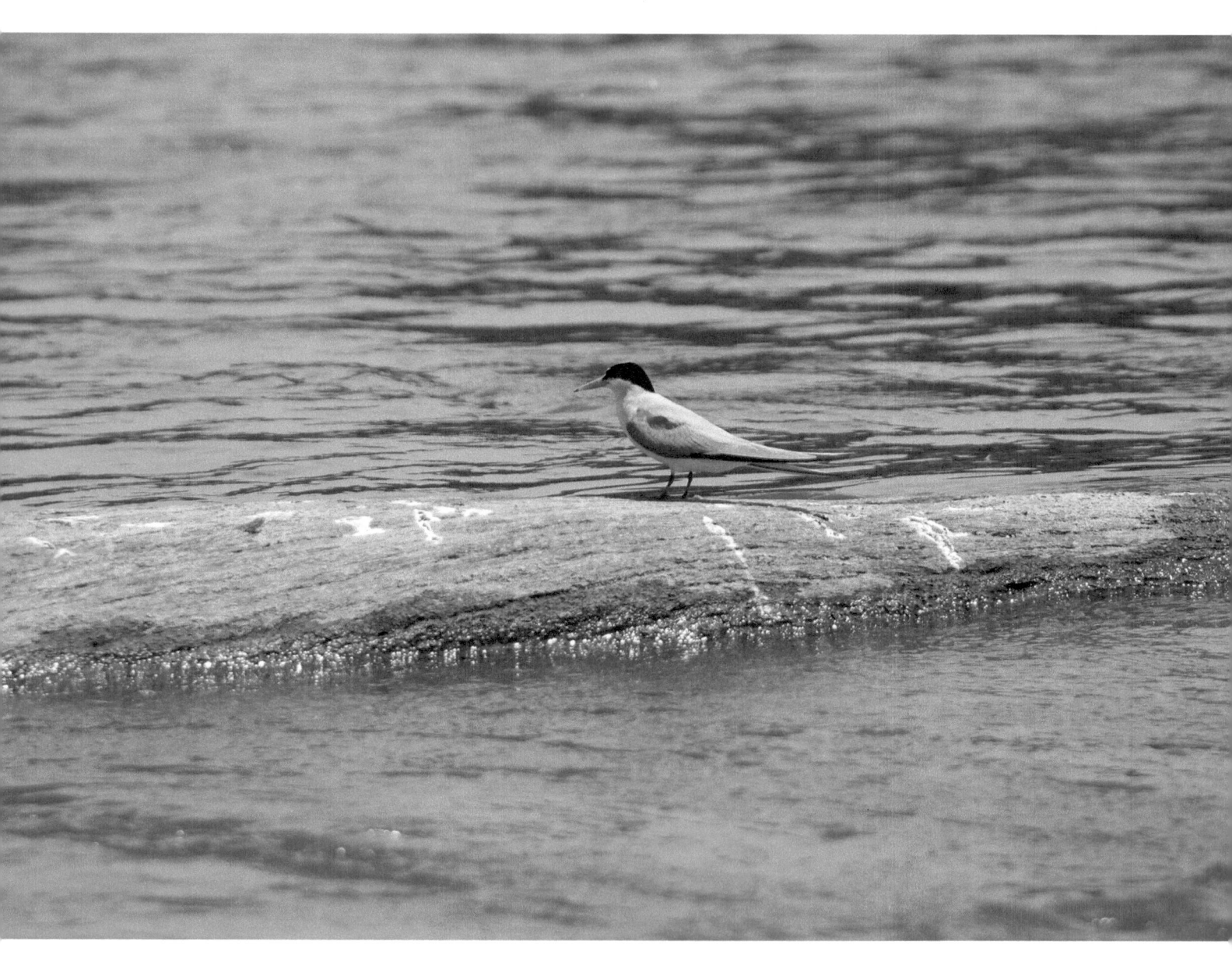

Least Tern resting
Segment 2, Johnson County

"BECAUSE OF ITS sandy substrate the river is always changing. In a sense it is unpredictable. Yet, this changeability is what makes it a critical habitat for two small populations of protected birds: the Least Tern and Piping Plover. The tern nests elsewhere in Kansas but for the Piping Plover, this is the only place."

- Roger L. Boyd

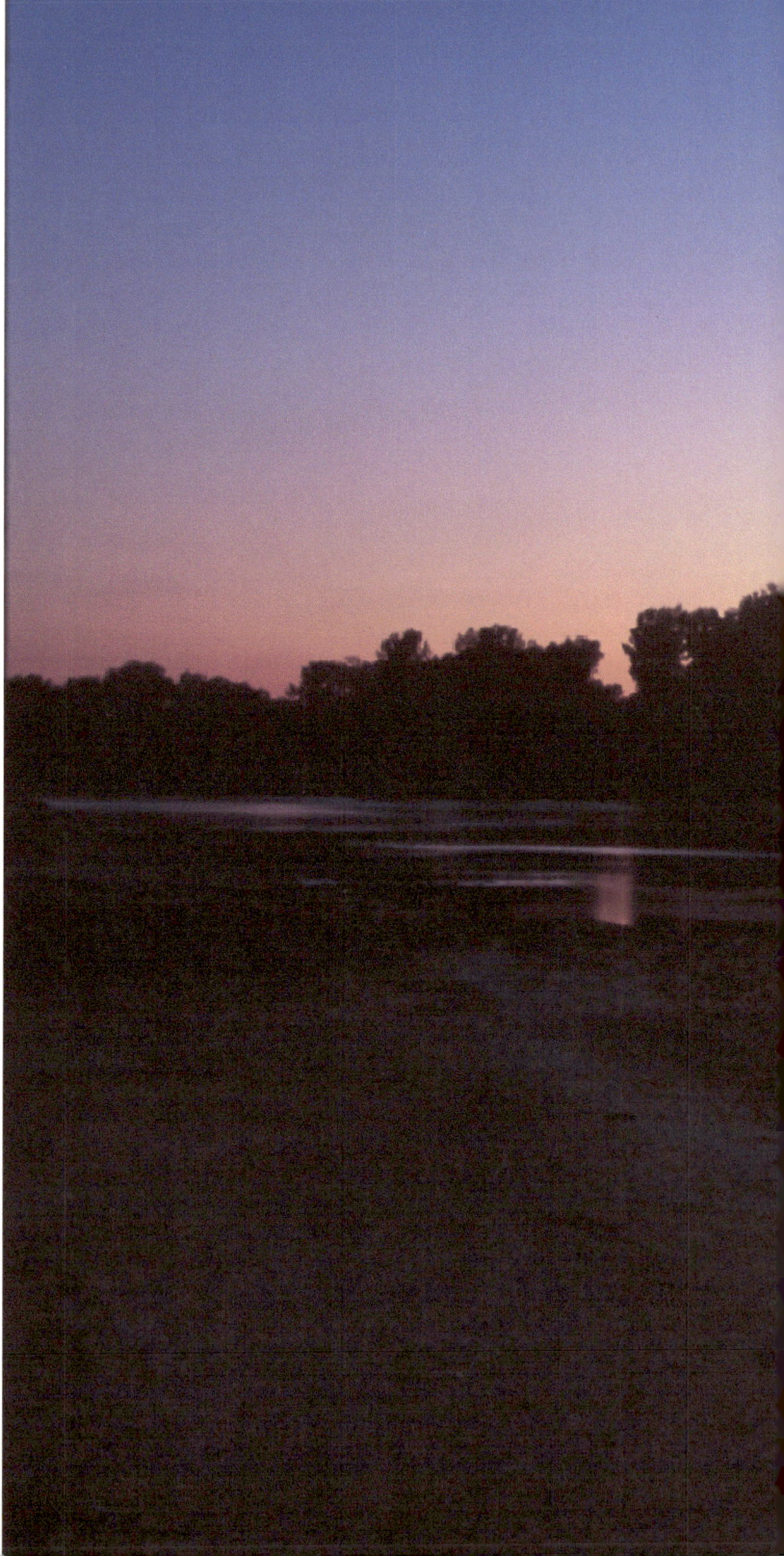

"IT IS AT NIGHT
that the Kaw chooses
to free itself. The sun,
the egrets, the willows,
the snags and your own
eyes lose their connection
to the water. And the
Kaw knows you're not
watching as it sheds its
nightly skin on its
snake-shaped path.**"**

130

- Christina Ruiz

Darkness falls on the Kaw
Segment 2, Wyandotte County

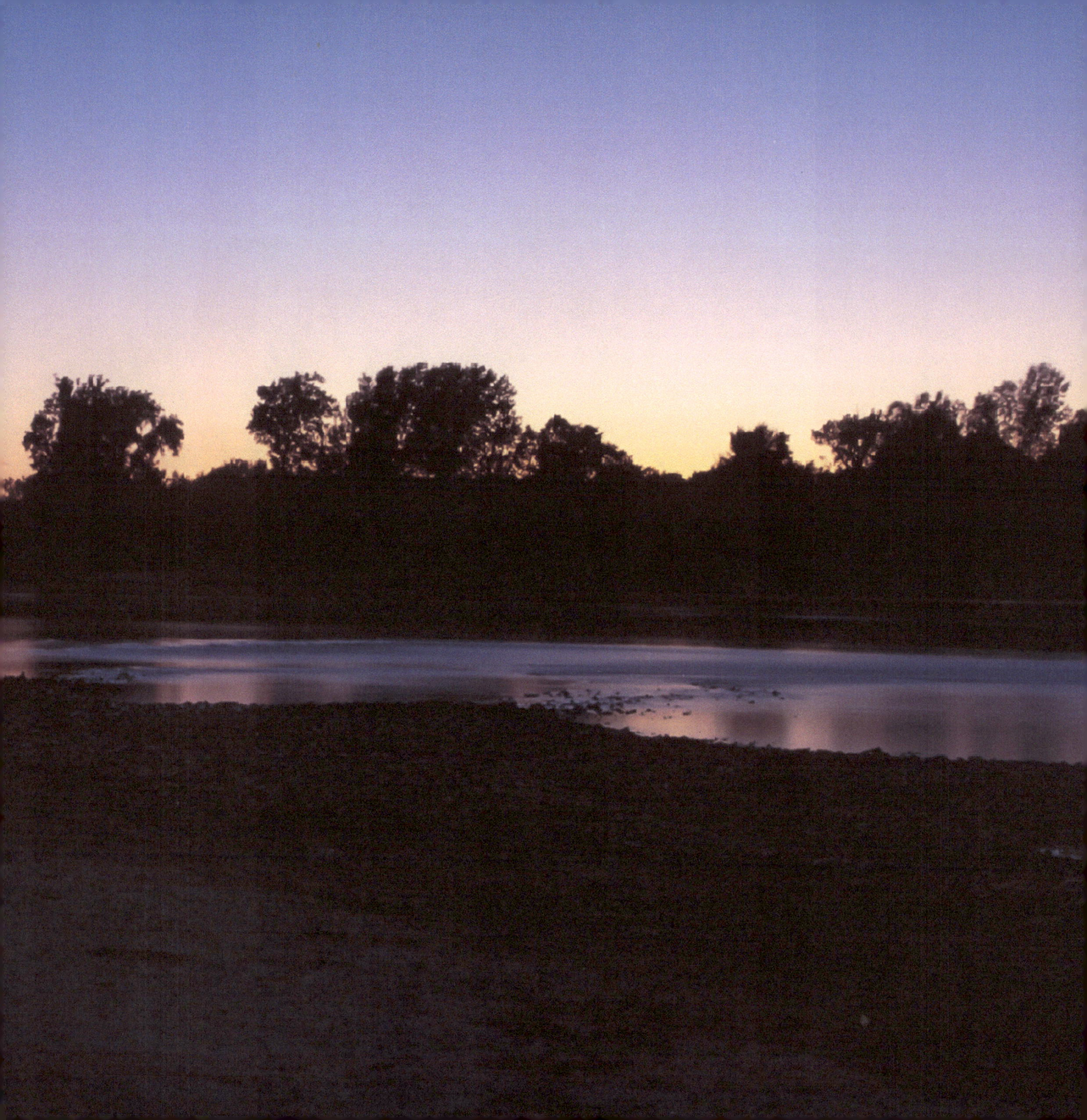

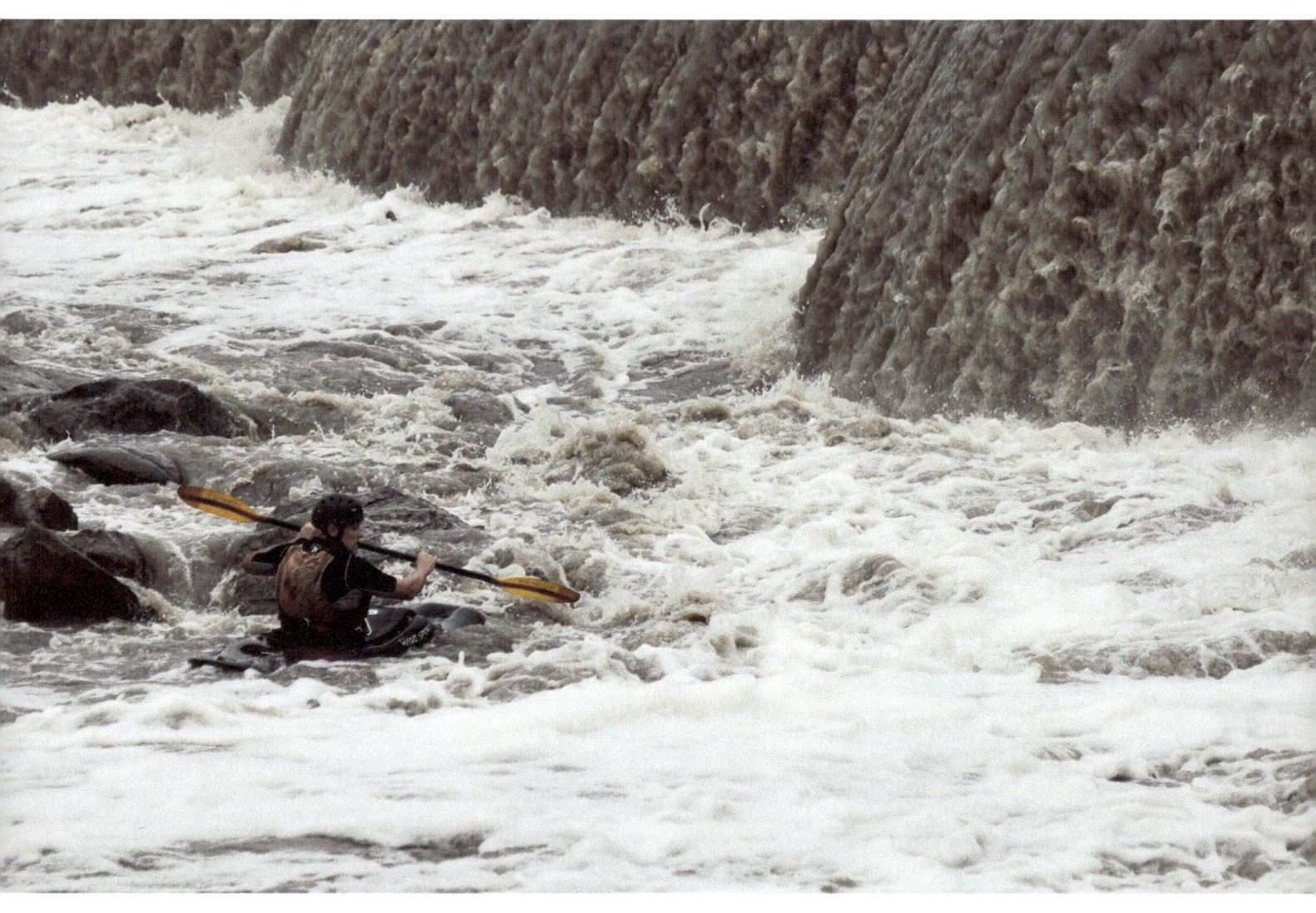

Whitewater kayaking at WaterOne weir
Segment 1, Johnson County

"THE WEIR at Johnson County is one of the best whitewater spots in the state of Kansas. We've always had fun paddling there.**"**

- David E. Bohannan

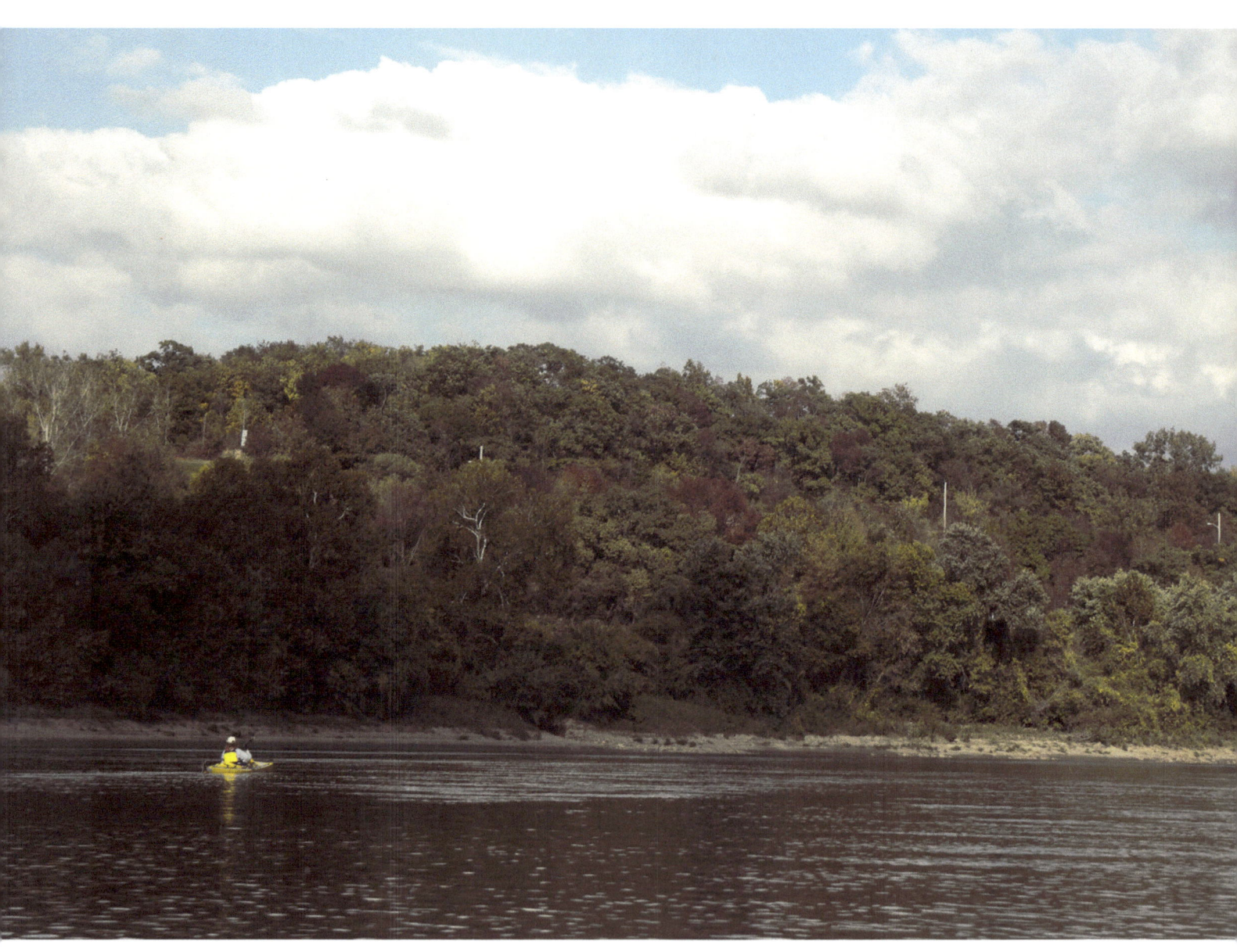

Early fall colors along the Kaw
Segment 1, Wyandotte County

"I GREW UP NEAR the Kaw River in Kansas City, KS and played along it from the time I was a young child. I continue to "play" in it by kayaking, canoeing and camping along it. It is a very beautiful river during all four of the seasons. The Kaw River holds a very special place in my heart and it will always be "The River" of my childhood."

- William (Tom) Stull

"MY LIFE SEEMS to be a quest to commune with nature so it certainly is a fit to float the Kaw and its tributaries."

- Marilynn Koelliker

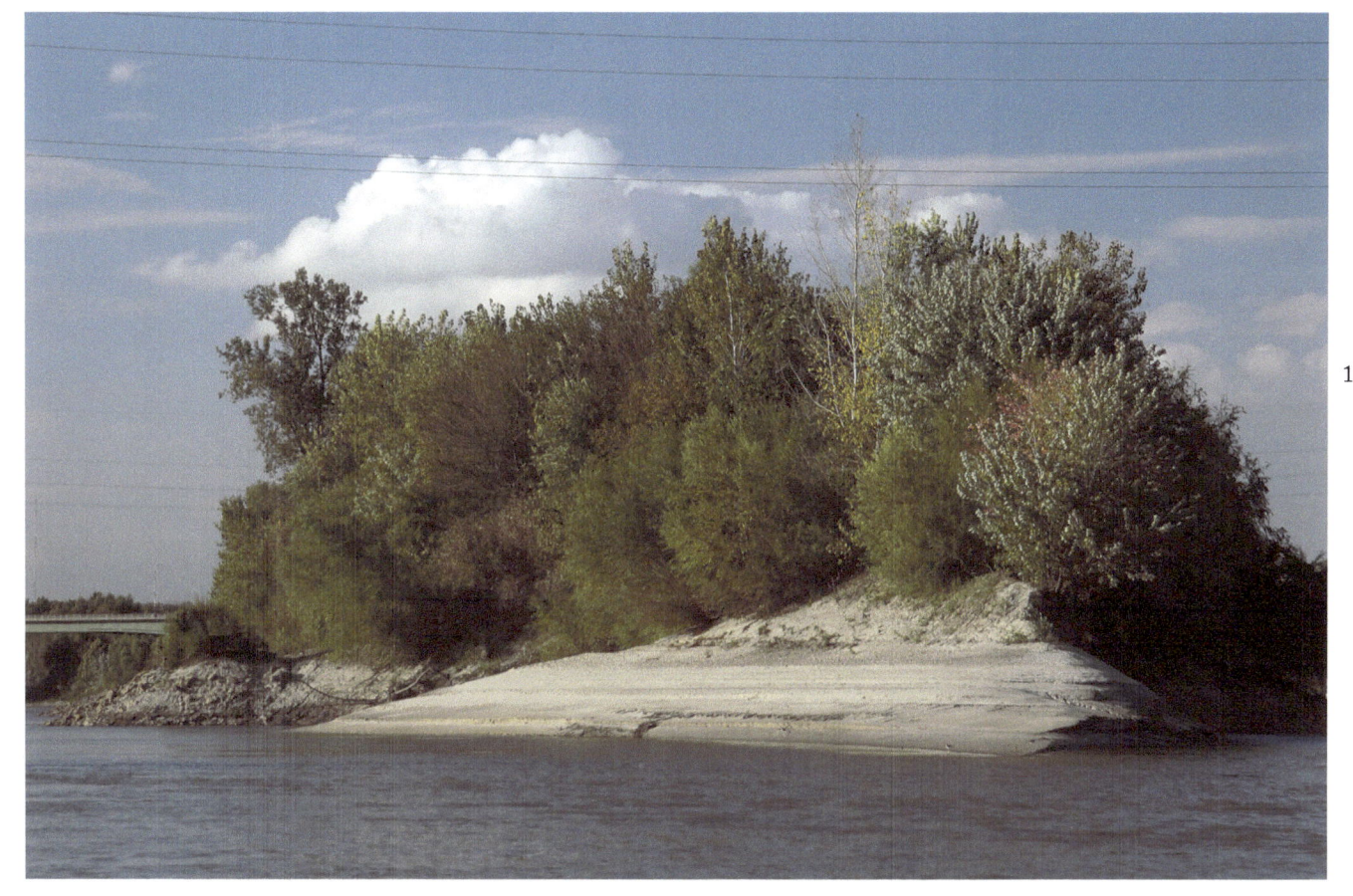

18th Street island
Segment 1, Wyandotte County

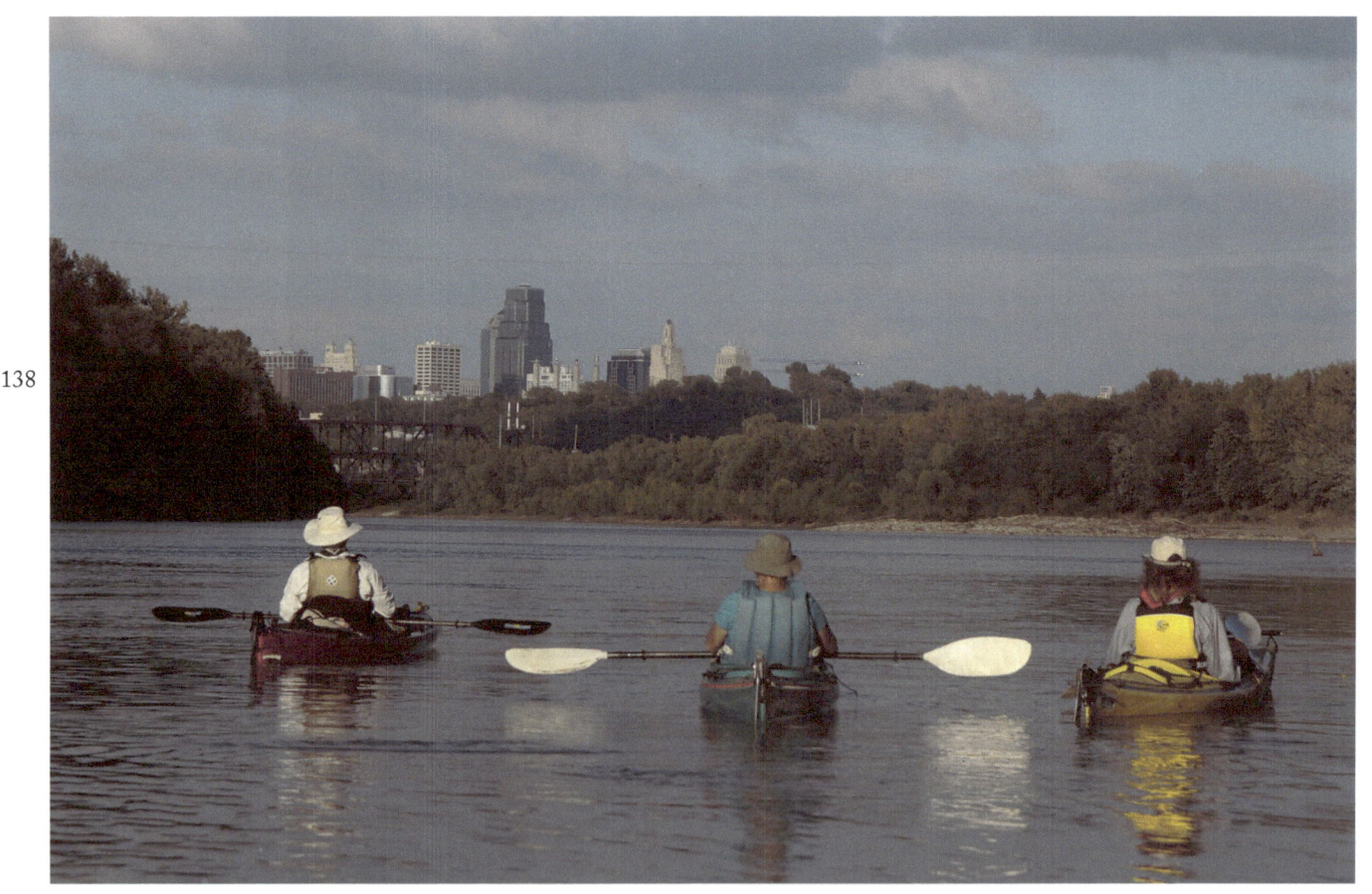

Downtown KCMO
Segment 1, Wyandotte County

"I LIVE 1 MILE down the river from Kaw Point in a loft in downtown Kansas City. Since I have no backyard, the Kaw River has become my back yard. I am on the water most every available night during the summer. The Kaw has become my recreational outlet and my training outlet. It gives me a calm and completely different view of Kansas City. It is definitely one of the best kept secrets in the Kansas City area."

-Doug Jennings

"FLOATING from Cedar Creek to Kaw Point gave me a new perspective of the many 'bridges of the kaw'. Every time I drive over to the "other side", fond memories return."

-Marsha Farley

140

Kansas Ave. Bridge and Kemper Arena
Segment 1, Wyandotte County

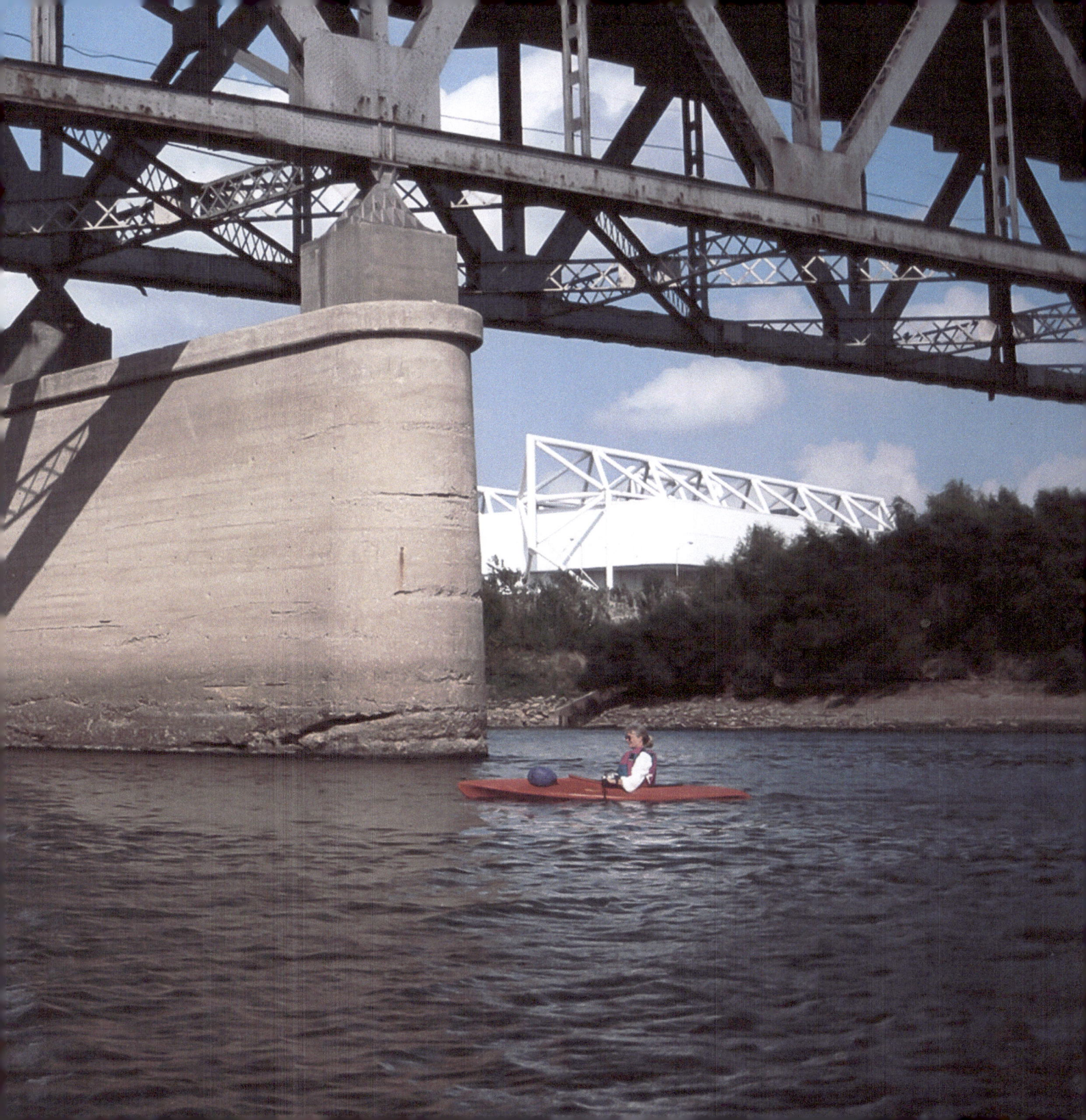

142

Strawberry Hill
Segment 1, Wyandotte County

(opposite)
Happy fisherman with catch
Segment 1, Wyandotte County

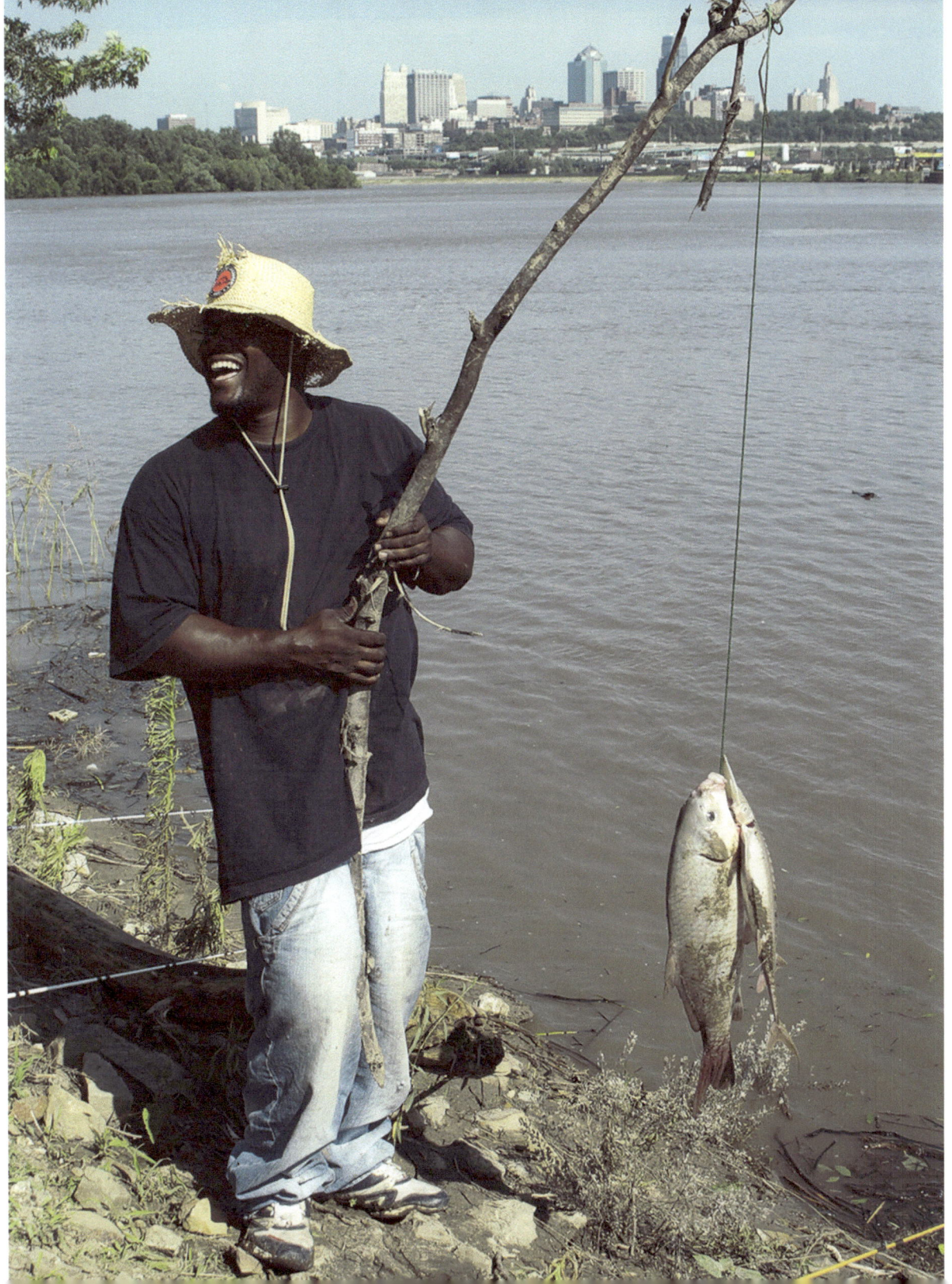

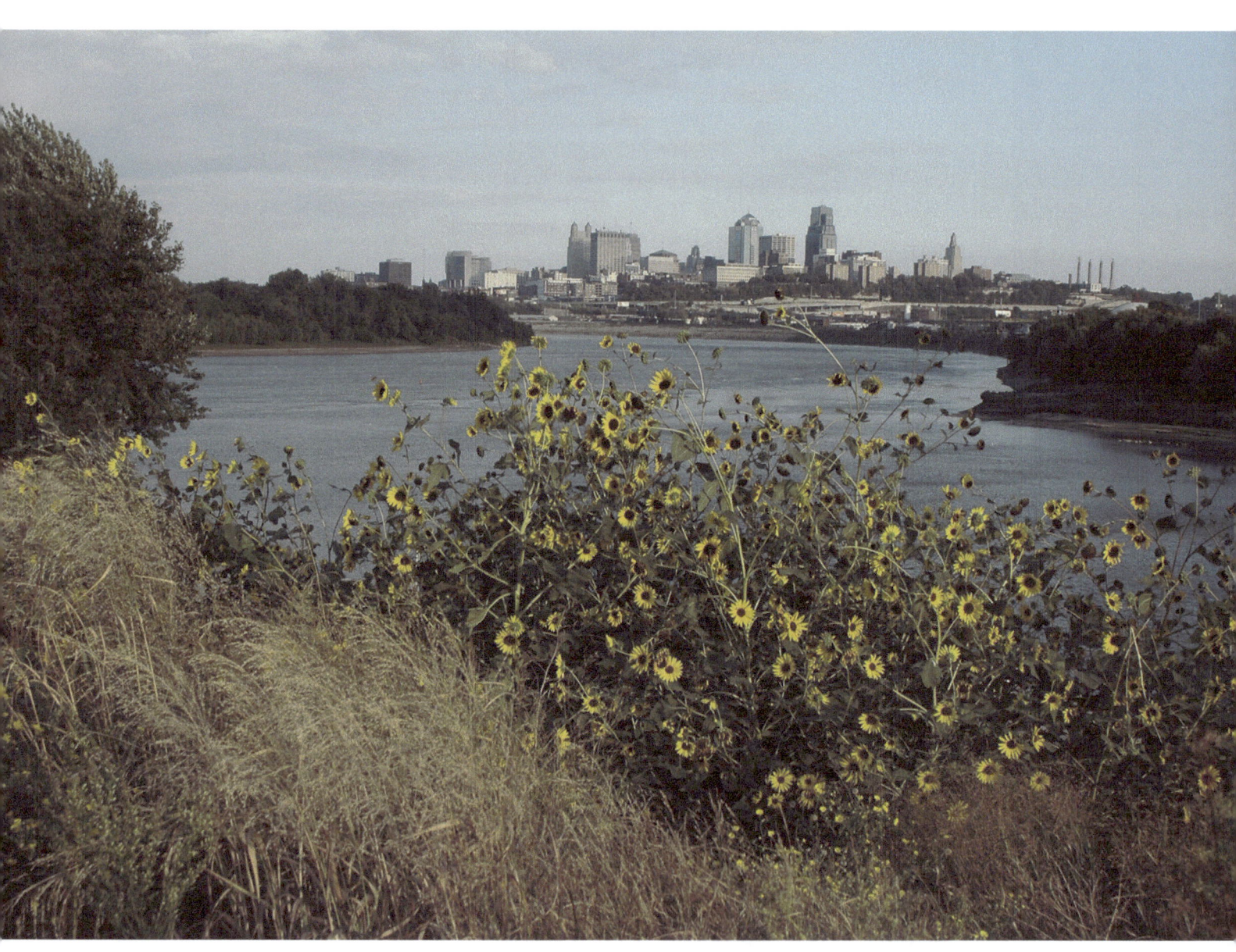

Late summer at Kaw Point
Segment 1, Wyandotte County

"THE KAW, our state river, holds water from the farthest reaches of western Kansas and blends it seamlessly with those waters of its bigger sister the Missouri.**"**

- Mike Hayden

(overleaf)
Early evening at Kaw Point
Segment 1, Wyandotte County

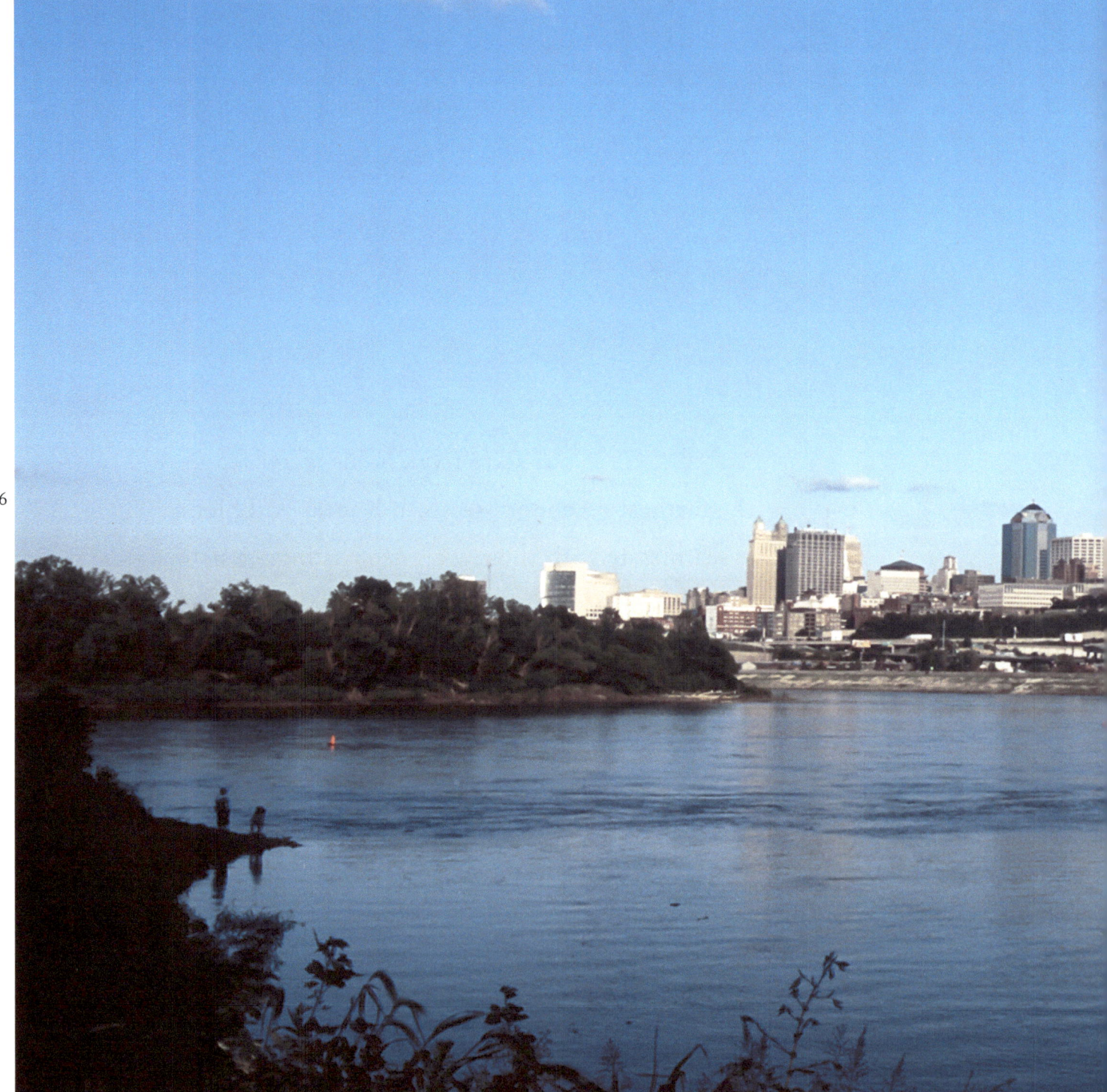

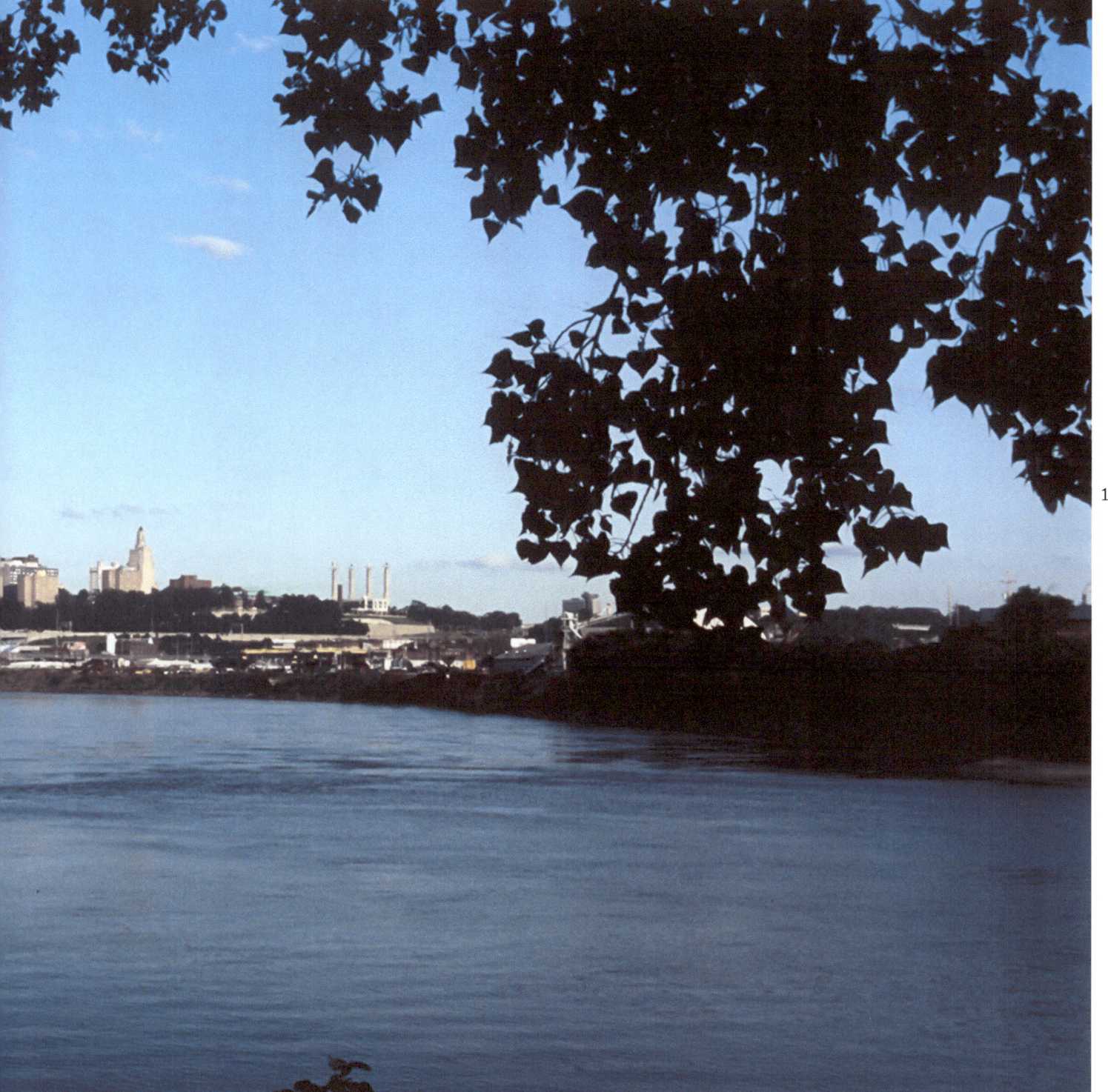

ACCESS ALONG

Tuttle Creek Lake

POTTAWATOMIE

JACKSON

RILEY

Milford Lake

Manhattan ⑤

St. George

Wamego

Belvue

St. Marys

Kansas

Rossville

Silver Lake

Ogden ③

④ ⑥

⑦

⑧ 24

⑨

⑩ River

18

Fort Riley

②

①

Junction City

Maple Hill

Willard ⑪

GEARY

WABAUNSEE

I-70

77

177

99

63

LEGEND

① = Grant Park Access (Republican River)

② = First Territorial Capitol SHS Park Trail

③ = Ogden Access

④ = Fairmont Park Access

⑤ = Linear Park Access (Blue River)

⑥ = Linear Park Trail (Kansas River)

⑦ = St. George Access

⑧ = Wamego Access

⑨ = Belvue Access

⑩ = Maple Hill Bridge Access

⑪ = Willard Access (Proposed)

⑫ = Kaw River State Park Access

⑬ = Topeka Water Department weir/portage

⑭ = Seward Avenue Access

⑮ = City of Perry Walking Nature Trail

THE KAW

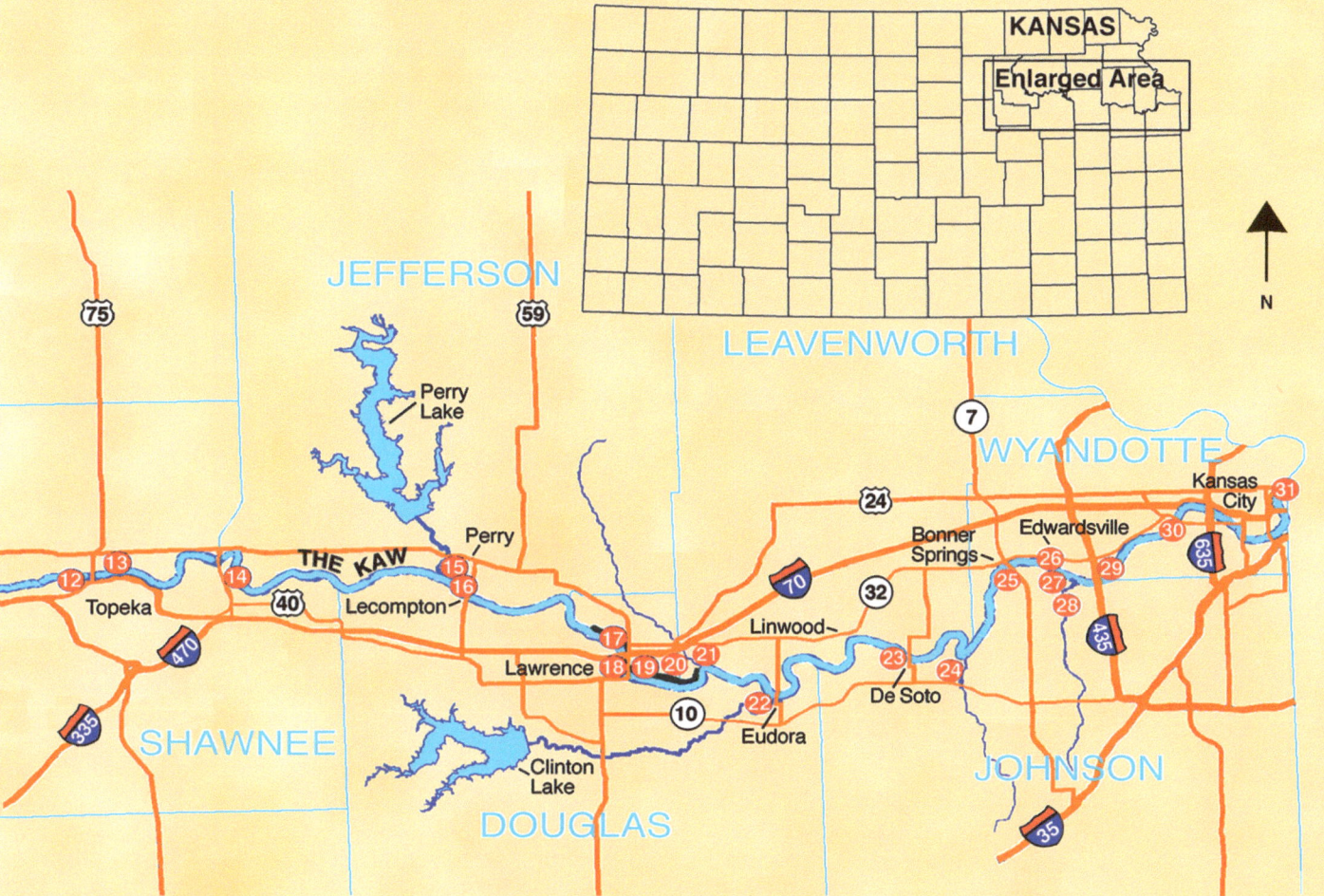

149

KANSAS

Enlarged Area

N

JEFFERSON

LEAVENWORTH

WYANDOTTE

Perry Lake

Kansas City

Perry

THE KAW

Bonner Springs

Edwardsville

Topeka

Lecompton

Linwood

Lawrence

De Soto

SHAWNEE

Clinton Lake

Eudora

JOHNSON

DOUGLAS

16 = Rising Sun Access

17 = Lawrence River Front Park Access

18 = Burcham and Constant Park Trails

19 = 8th Street Access

20 = Levee Trail and River Trail

21 = Mud Creek Tributary Access

22 = Eudora Access (Wakarusa River)

23 = De Soto Access

24 = Cedar Creek Tributary Access

25 = Shawnee Access (Proposed)

26 = Edwardsville Access

27 = Nelson Island

28 = Mill Creek Tributary Access

29 = Johnson County Waterone weir/portage

30 = Turner Bridge Access

31 = Kaw Point Access

Index To Contributing Authors

The following sources are gratefully acknowledge: Page 24 from "Canoeing the Kaw" by Mike Calwell in *KANSAS!* magazine, fall issue, 1999; Page 40 from "Member Profile, Carey Maynard-Moody" in *Kansas River Currents*, May 2005; Page 34, 92 from "Comments on the Esthetic Value of the River" by Mike Ducey in *Corps of Engineers Victory Sand and Gravel Hearing*, May 1995; Page 125 from "Me and Faraji on the Kaw" by Stephen Garlow in *The Kansas Trails Council*, Vol. XXIX No. 4, January 2004.

Craig Thompson is a scientist with the U.S. Environmental Protection Agency (EPA). This book was approved for publication following US EPA Policy. Mention of commercial products or trade names does not constitute endorsement or recommendation for use.

Mr. Thompson's photographs have appeared in *KANSAS!* magazine, *Paddling Kansas, Exploring the Kaw Valley, Forever Kansas!,* and other publications. His photographs also appeared in many *KANSAS!* magazine calendars and a front cover for the magazine's 1995 fiftieth anniversary issue. Several of the images in this book are available as beautiful Kaw River cards. To ask for more information about purchasing these cards, please go to cthompsun@gmail.com.

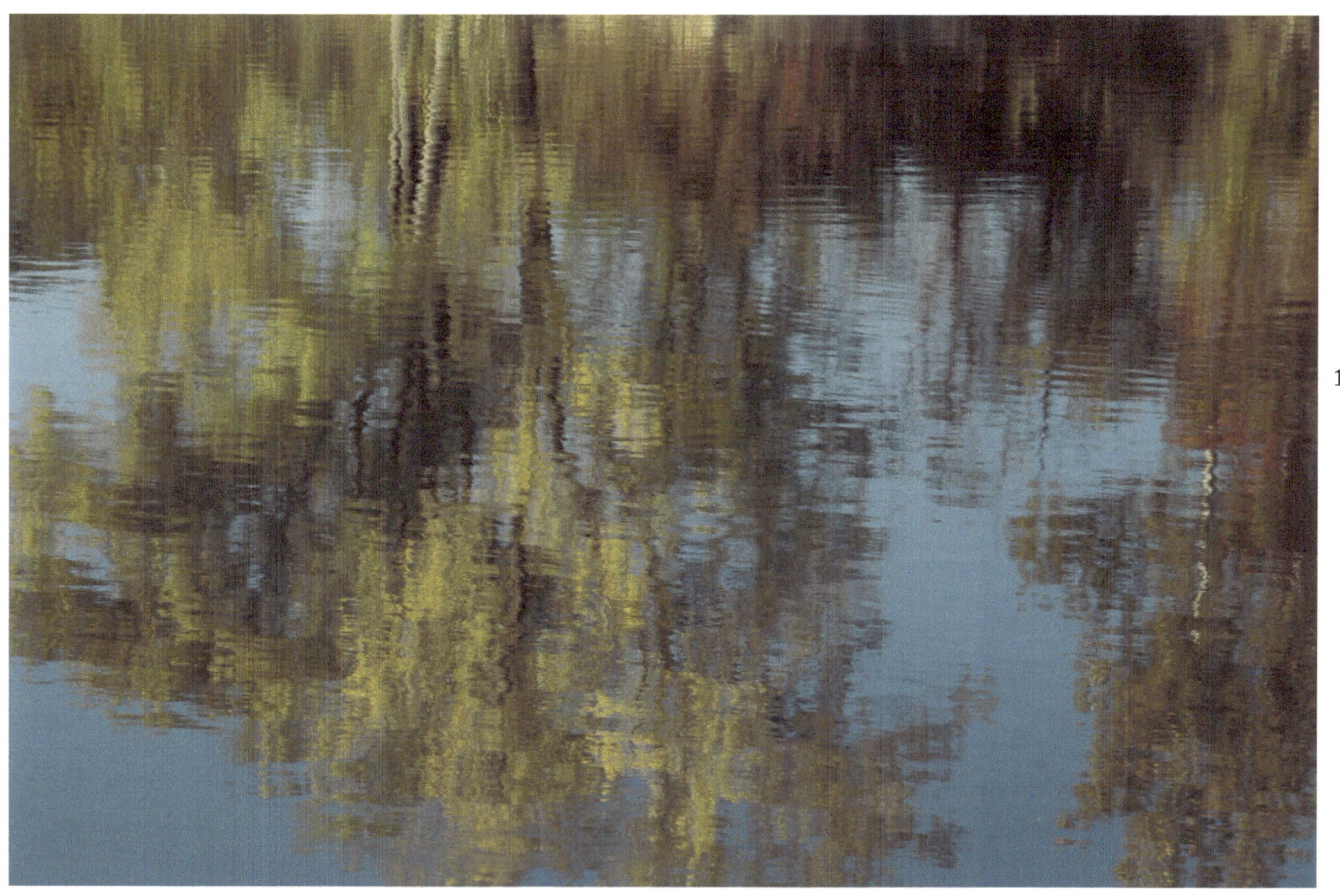

153

Cottonwood tree in fall reflection
Segment 19, Leavenworth County

www.ingramcontent.com/pod-product-compliance
Lightning Source LLC
Chambersburg PA
CBHW050715180526
45159CB00003B/1031